Trial of the W: the Resurrection of Jesus

Thomas Sherlock

Alpha Editions

This edition published in 2024

ISBN : 9789362099402

Design and Setting By
Alpha Editions
www.alphaedis.com
Email - info@alphaedis.com

Contents

THE TRIAL OF THE WITNESSES
OF THE RESURRECTION OF JESUS

We were, not long since, some Gentlemen of the inns of court together, each to other so well known, that no man's presence was a confinement to any other, from speaking his mind on any subject that happened to arise in conversation. The meeting was without design, and the discourse, as in like cases, various. Among other things we fell upon the subject of Woolston's trial and conviction, which had happened some few days before. That led to a debate, How the law finds in such cases? what punishment it inflicts? and, in general, whether the law ought at all to interpose in controversies of this kind? We were not agreed in these points. One, who maintained the favorable side to Woolston, discovered a great liking and approbation of his discourses against the miracles of Christ, and seemed to think his arguments unanswerable. To which another replied, I wonder that one of your abilities, and bred to the profession of the law, which teaches us to consider the nature of evidence, and its proper weight, can be of that opinion: I am sure you would be unwilling to determine a property of five shillings upon such evidence, as you now think material enough to overthrow the miracles of Christ.

It may easily be imagined, that this opened a door to much dispute, and determined the conversation for the remainder of the evening to this subject. The dispute ran thro' almost all the particulars mentioned in Woolston's pieces; but the thread of it was broken by several digressions, and the pursuit of things which were brought accidentally into the discourse. At length one of the company said pleasantly; Gentlemen, you don't argue like lawyers; if I were judge in this cause, I would hold you better to the point. The company took the hint, and cried, they should be glad to have the cause reheard, and him to be the judge. The Gentlemen who had engaged with mettle and spirit in a dispute which arose accidentally, seemed very unwilling to be drawn into a formal controversy; and especially the Gentleman who argued against Woolston, thought the matter grew too serious for him, and excused himself from undertaking a controversy in religion, of all others the most momentous. But he was told, that the argument should be confined merely to the nature of the evidence; and that might be considered, without entering into any such controversy as he would avoid; and, to bring the matter within bounds, and under one view, the evidence of Christ's resurrection, and the exceptions taken to it, should be the only subject of the conference. With such persuasion he suffered himself to be persuaded, and promised to give the company, and their new-made judge, a meeting that day fortnight. The judge and the rest of the company were for bringing on the cause a week sooner; but the council for Woolston took the matter up, and said, Consider, Sir, the Gentleman is not to argue out of Littleton, Plowden, or Coke, authors to him well known; but he must have his authorities from Matthew, Mark, Luke, and John; and a fortnight is time little enough of all conscience to gain a familiarity with a new acquaintance: and, turning to the Gentleman, he said, I'll call upon you before the fortnight is out, to see how reverend an appearance you make behind Hammond on the New Testament, a concordance on one hand, and a folio Bible with references on the other. You shall be welcome, Sir, replied the Gentleman; and perhaps you may find some company more to your own taste. He is but a poor council who studies on one side of the question only; and therefore I will have your friend Woolston, T____l, and C___s, to entertain you when you do me the favor of the visit. Upon this we parted in good humour, and all pleased with the appointment made, except the two Gentlemen who were to provide the entertainment.

The Second Day

The company met at the time appointed: but as it happened in this, as in like cases it often does, that some friends to some of the company, who were not of the party the first day, had got notice of the meeting; and the Gentlemen who were to debate the question, found they had a more numerous audience than they expected or desired. He especially who was to maintain the evidence for the resurrection, began to excuse the necessity he was under of disappointing their expectation, alledging that he was not prepared; and he had persisted in excusing himself, but that the strangers who perceived what the case was, offered to withdraw; which the Gentleman would by no means consent to: they insisting to go, he said, he would much rather submit himself to their candour, unprepared as he was, than be guilty of such rudeness, as to force them to leave the company. Upon which one of the company, smiling, said, It happens luckily that our number is increased: when we were last together, we appointed a judge, but we quite forgot a jury: and now, I think, we are good men and true, sufficient to make one. This thought was pursued in several allusions to legal proceedings; which created some mirth, and had this good effect, that it dispersed the solemn air, which the mutual compliments upon the difficulty before mentioned had introduced, and restored the ease and good humour natural to the conversation of Gentlemen.

The judge perceiving the disposition of the company, thought it a proper time to begin, and called out, Gentlemen of the jury, take your places; and immediately seated himself at the upper end of the table. The company sat round him, and the judge called upon the council for Woolston to begin.

Mr. A. Council for Woolston, addressing himself to the judge, said,

May it please your Lordship, I conceive the Gentleman on the other side ought to begin, and lay his evidence, which he intends to maintain, before the court; till that is done, it is to no purpose for me to object. I amy perhaps object to something which he will not admit to be any part of his evidence; and therefore I apprehend, the evidence ought in the first place to be distinctly stated.

Judge. Mr. B What say you to that?

Mr. B. Council on the other side:

My Lord, If the evidence I am to maintain, were to suppose any new claim; if I were to gain any thing which I am not already possessed of, the Gentleman would be in the right: but the evidence is old, and is matter of record; and I have been long in possession of all that I claim under it. If the Gentleman has anything to say to dispossess me, let him produce it; otherwise I have no reason to bring my own title into question. And this I take to be the known method of proceeding in such cases: no man is obliged to produce his title to his possession; it is sufficient if he maintain it when it is called in question.

Mr A. Surely, my Lord, the Gentleman mistakes the case. I can never admit myself to be out of possession of my understanding and reason; and since he would put me out of this possession, and compel me to admit things incredible, in virtue of the evidence he maintains, he ought to set forth his claim, or leave the world to be directed by common sense.

Judge. Sir, you say right, upon supposition that the truth of the Christian religion were the point in question. In that case it would be necessary to produce the evidence for the Christian religion. But the matter now before the court is, Whether the objections produced by Mr. Woolston, are of weight to overthrow the evidence of Christ's resurrection? You see then the evidence of the resurrection is supposed to be what it is on both sides; and the thing immediately in judgement is, the value of the objections; and therefore they must be set forth. The court will be bound to take notice of the evidence, which is admitted as a fact on both parts. Go on, Mr. A.

Mr. A. My Lord, I submit to the direction of the court, I cannot but observe, that the Gentleman on the other side, unwilling as he seems to be to state his evidence, did not forget to lay in his claim to prescription; which is perhaps, in truth, tho' he has too much skill to own it, the very strength of his cause. I do allow, that the Gentleman maintains nothing, but what his father and grandfather, and his ancestors, beyond time of man's memory, maintained before him: I allow too, that prescription in many cases makes a good title; but it must always be with this condition, that the thing is capable of being prescribed for: and I insist, that prescription cannot run against reason and common sense. Customs may be pleaded by prescription; but if, upon showing the custom, anything unreasonable appears in it, the prescription fails; for length of time works nothing towards the establishing anything that could never have a legal commencement. And if this objection will overthrow all prescriptions for customs; the mischief of which extends perhaps to one poor village only, and affects them in no greater a concern, than their right of common upon a ragged mountain: shall it not much more prevail, when the interest of mankind is concerned, and in no less a point than his happiness in this life, and all his hopes for futurity? Besides, if prescription must be allowed in this case, how will you deal with it in others? What will you say to the ancient Persians, and their fire-altars? nay, what to the Turks, who have been long enough in possession of their faith to plead ———-

Mr. B. I beg pardon for interrupting the Gentleman, but it is to save him trouble. He is going into his favorite common-place, and has brought us from Persia to Turkey already; and if he goes on, I know we must follow him around the globe. To save us from this long journey, I'll waive all advantage from the antiquity of the resurrection, and the general reception the belief of it has found in the world; and am content to consider it as a fact which happened but last year, and was never heard of either by the Gentleman's grandfather, or by mine.

Mr. A. I should not have taken quite so long a journey as the Gentleman imagines; nor, indeed, need any man go far from home to find instances to the purpose I was upon. But, since this advantage is quitted, I am as willing to spare my pains, as the Gentleman is desirous that I should. And yet I suspect some art even in this concession, fair and candid as it seems to be. For I am persuaded, that one reason, perhaps the main reason, why men believe this history of Jesus, is, that they cannot conceive, that any one should attempt, much less succeed in such an attempt as this, upon the foundation of mere human cunning and policy; and 'tis worth to go round the globe, as the Gentleman expressed himself, so see various instances of the like kind, in order to remove this prejudice. But I stand corrected, and will go directly to the point now in judgement.

Mr. B. My Lord, the Gentleman, in justification of his first argument, has entered upon another of a very different kind. I think he is sensible of it, and seeming to yield up one of his popular topicks, is indeed artfully getting rid of another; which has made a very good figure in many late writings, but will not bear in any place where he who maintains it may be asked questions. The mere antiquity of the resurrection I gave up; for, if the evidence was not good at first, it can't be good now. The Gentleman is willing, he says, to spare us his history of ancient errors; and intimates, that upon this account he passes over many instances of fraud, that were in like circumstances to the case before us. I would not have the main strength of his case betrayed in complaisance to me. Nothing can be more material than to show a fraud of this kind, that prevailed universally in the world. Christ Jesus declared himself a Prophet, and put the proof of his mission on this, that he should die openly and publickly, and rise again the third day. This surely was the hardest plot in the world to be managed; and if there be one instance of this kind, or in any degree like it, by all means let it be produced.

Mr. A. My Lord, There has hardly been an instance of a false religion in the world, but it has also afforded a like instance to this before us. Have they not all pretended to inspiration? Upon what foot did Pythagoras, Numa, and others set up? Did they not all converse with the gods, and pretend to deliver oracles?

Mr. B. This only shews, that revelation is by the common consent of mankind the very best foundation of religion; and therefore every imposter pretends to it. But is a man's hiding himself in a cave for some years, and then coming out into the world, to be compared to a man's dying, and rising to life again? So far from it, that you and I and every man may do the one, but no man can do the other.

Mr. A. Sir, I suppose it will be allowed to be as great a thing to go to heaven, and converse with angels, and with God, and to come down to earth again, as it is to die, and rise again? Now, this very thing Mahomet pretended to do; and all his disciples believe it. Can you deny this fact?

Mr. B. Deny it, Sir? No. But tell us who went with Mahomet? Who were his witnesses? I expect, before we are done, to hear of the guards set over the sepulchre of Christ, and the seal of the stone. What guard watched Mahomet in his going or returning? What seals and credentials had he? He himself pretends to none. His followers pretend to nothing but his own word. We are now to consider the evidence for Christ's resurrection, and you think to parallel it, by producing a case for which no one ever pretended there was any evidence. You have Mahomet's word; and no man ever told a lie, but you had his word for the truth of what he said: and therefore you need not go round the globe to find such instances as these. But this story, it is said, has gained great credit, and is received by many nations. Very well. And how was it received? Was not every man converted to this faith with the sword at his throat? In our case, every witness to the resurrection, and every believer of it, was hourly exposed to death. In the other case, whoever refused to believe, died; or, what was as bad, lived a wretched conquered slave. And will you pretend these cases to be alike? One case indeed there was, within our own memory, which, in some circumstances, came near to the case now before us. The French prophets put the credit of their mission upon the resurrection of Dr. Emmes, and gave publick notice of it. If the Gentleman pleases to make use of this instance, it is at his service.

Mr. A. The instance of Dr. Emmes is so far to the purpose, that it shews to what lengths enthusiasm will carry men. And why might not the same thing happen at Jerusalem, which happened but a few years ago in our own country? Matthew and John, and the rest of them, managed that affair with more dexterity than the French prophets; so that the resurrection of Jesus gained credit in the world, and the French prophets sunk under their ridiculous pretensions. That is all the difference.

Mr. B. Is it so? And a very wide difference, I promise you. In one case everything happened that was proper to convince the world of the resurrection; in the other, the event manifested the cheat: and upon the view of these circumstances, you think it is sufficient to say, with great coolness, That is all the difference. Why, what difference do you expect between truth and falsehood? What distinction _____

Judge. Gentlemen, you forget you are in a court, and are falling into dialogue. Courts don't allow of chit-chat. Look ye, the evidence of the resurrection of Jesus is before the court, recorded by Matthew, Mark, and others. You must take it as it is; you can neither make it better, or worse. These witnesses are accused of giving false evidence. Come to the point; and let us hear what you have to offer to prove the accusation.

Mr. B. Is it your meaning, Sir, that the objections should be stated and argued all together, and that the answer should be to the whole at once? or would you have the objections argued singly, and answered separately by themselves?

Judge. I think this court may dispense with the strict forms of legal proceeding; and therefore I leave this to the choice of the jury.

After the jury had consulted together, the foreman rose up,

The Foreman of the Jury. We desire to hear the objections argued and answered separately. We shall be better able to form a judgement, by hearing the answer while the objection is fresh in our minds.

Judge. Gentlemen, you hear the opinion of the jury. Go on.

Mr. A I am now to disclose to you a scene, of all others the most surprising. "The resurrection has been long talked of, and, to the amazement of everyone who can think freely, has been believed through all ages of the church." This general and constant belief creates in most minds a presumption that it was founded on good evidence. In other cases the evidence supports the credit of the history; but here the evidence itself is presumed only upon the credit which the story has gained. I wish the books dispersed against Jesus by the ancient Jews had not been lost; for they would have given us a clear insight into this contrivance: but it is happy for us, that the very account given by the pretended witnesses of this fact, is sufficient to destroy the credit of it.

The resurrection was not a thing contrived for its own sake. No! it was undertaken to support great views, and for the sake of great consequences that were to attend it. It will be necessary therefore to lay before you those views, that you may be the better judge of this part of the contrivance, when you have the whole scene before you.

The Jews were a weak superstitious people, and, as is common among such people, gave great credit to some traditionary prophecies about their own country. They had, besides, some old books among them, which they esteemed to be writings of certain Prophets, who had formerly lived among them, and whose memory they had in great veneration. From such old books and traditions they formed many extravagant expectations; and among the rest one was, that some time or other a great victorious prince would rise among them, and subdue all their enemies, and make them lords of the world. In Augustus's time they were in a low state, reduced under the Roman yoke; and as they never wanted a deliverer more, so the eagerness of this hope, as it happens to weak minds, turned into a firm expectation that he would soon come. This proved a temptation to some bold, and to some cunning men, to personate the prince so much expected. And "nothing is more natural and common to promote rebellions, than to ground them on new prophecies, or new interpretations of old ones; prophecies being suited to the vulgar superstition, and operating with the force of religion." Accordingly, many such imposters rose, pretending to be the victorious prince expected; and they, and the people who followed them, perished in the folly of their attempt.

But Jesus, knowing that victories and triumphs are not things to be counterfeited; that the people were not to be delivered from the Roman yoke by sleight of hand; and having no hope of being able to cope with the Emperor of Rome in good earnest, took another and more successful method to carry on his design. He took upon him to be the prince foretold in the ancient Prophets; but then he insisted that the true sense of the prophecies had been mistaken; that they related not to the kingdoms of this world, but to the kingdom of heaven; that the Messias was not to be a conquering prince, but a suffering one; that he was not to come with horses of war, and chariots of war, but was to be meek and lowly, riding on an ass. By this means, he got the common and necessary foundation for a new revelation, which is to be built and founded on a precedent revelation.

To carry on this design, he made choice of twelve men of no fortunes or education, and of such understandings, as gave no jealousy that they would discover the plot. And, what is most wonderful, and shews their ability, while the master was preaching the kingdom of heaven, these poor men, not weaned from the prejudices of their country, expected every day that he would declare himself a king, and were quarreling who should be his first minister. This expectation had a good effect on the service; for it kept them constant to their master.

I must observe further, that the Jews were under strange apprehensions of supernatural powers: and as their own religion was founded on the belief of certain miracles said to be wrought by their lawgiver Moses; so were they ever running after wonders and miracles, and ready to take up with any stories of this kind. Now, as something extraordinary was necessary to support the pretensions of Jesus, he dextrously laid hold of this weakness of the people, and set up to be a wonder-worker. His disciples were well qualified to receive this impression: they saw, or thought they saw many strange things, and were able to spread the fame and report of them abroad.

This conduct had the desired success. The whole country was alarmed, and full of the news of a great Prophet's being come among them. They were too full of their own imagination, to attend to the notion of a kingdom of heaven. Here was one mighty in deed and in word; and they concluded that he was the very prince their nation expected. Accordingly they once attempted to set him up for a King; and at another time attended him in triumph to Jerusalem. This natural consequence opens the natural design of the attempt. If things had gone on successfully to the end, it is probable that the kingdom of heaven would have been changed into a kingdom of this world. The design indeed failed, by the impatience and over-hastiness of the multitude; which alarmed not only the chief of the Jews, but the Roman governor also.

The case being come to this point, and Jesus seeing that he could not escape being put to death, he declared, that the ancient Prophets had foretold, that the Messias should die upon a cross, and that he should rise again on the third day. Here was the foundation for the continuing this plot, which otherwise had died with its author. This was his legacy to his followers; which, having been well managed by them and their successors, has at last produced a kingdom indeed; a kingdom of priests, who have governed the world for many ages, and have been strong enough to set Kings and Emperors at defiance. But so it happens, the ancient Prophets appealed to are still extant; and there being no such prophecies of the death and resurrection of the Messias, they are a standing evidence against this story. As he expected, so it happened, that he died on a cross; and the prosecuting of this contrivance was left to the management of his disciples and followers. Their part is next to be considered———.

Mr. B. My Lord, Since it is your opinion that the objections should be considered singly, and the Gentleman has carried his scheme down to the death of Christ, I think he is come to a proper rest; and that it is agreeable to your intention that I should be admitted to answer.

Judge. You say right, Sir. Let us hear what you answer to this charge.

Mr. B. My Lord, I was unwilling to disturb the Gentleman by breaking in upon his scheme; otherwise I would have reminded him that this court sits to examine evidence, and not to be entertained with fine imaginations. You have had a scheme laid before you, but not one bit of evidence to support any part of it; no, not so much as a pretence to any evidence. The Gentleman was, I remember, very sorry that the old books of the Jews were lost, which would, as he supposes, have set forth all this matter; and I agree with him, that he has much reason to be sorry, considering his great scarcity of proof. And since I have mentioned this, that I may not be to return to it again, I would ask the Gentleman now, how he knows there ever were such books? And since, if ever there were any, they are lost, how he knows what they contained? I doubt I shall have frequent occasion to ask such questions. It would indeed be a sufficient answer to the whole, to repeat the several suppositions that have been made, and to call for the evidence upon which they stand. This would plainly discover every part of the story to be mere fiction. But since the Gentleman seems to have endeavored to bring under one view the many insinuations which have of late been spread abroad by different hands, and to work the whole into a consistent scheme; I will, if your patience shall permit, examine this plot, and see to whom the honour of the contrivance belongs.

The Gentleman begins with expressing his "amazement, that the resurrection has been believed in all ages of the church." If you ask him, Why? he must answer , Because the account of it is a forgery; for it is no amazement to him, surely, that a true account should be generally well received. So that this remark proceeds indeed from confidence rather than amazement; and comes only to this, that he is sure that there was no resurrection. And I am sure that this is no evidence that there was none. Whether he is mistaken in his confidence, or I in mine, the court must judge.

The Gentleman's observation, That the general belief of the resurrection creates a presumption that it stands upon good evidence, and therefore people look no farther, but follow their fathers, as their fathers did their grandfathers before them, is in great measure true; but it is a truth nothing to his purpose. He allows, that the resurrection has been believed in all ages of the church; that is, from the very time of the resurrection: what then prevailed with those who first received it? They certainly did not follow the example of their fathers. Here then is the point, How did this fact gain credit in the world at first? Credit it has gained without doubt. If the multitude at present go into this belief through prejudice, example, and for company sake, they do in this case no more, nor otherwise, than they do in all cases. And it cannot be denied, but that truth may be received through prejudice, (as it is called), i.e. without examining the proof, or merits of the cause, as well as falsehood. What general truth is there, the merits of which all the world, or the one hundredth part has examined? It is smartly said somewhere, That the priest only continues what the nurse began. But the life of the remark consists in the quaintness of the antithesis between the nurse and the priest; and owes its support much more to sound than to sense. For is it possible that children should not hear something of the common and popular opinions of their country, whether these opinions be true or false? Do they not learn the common maxims of reason this way? Perhaps every man first learned from his nurse that two and two make four; and whenever she divides an apple among her children, she instills into them this prejudice, That the whole is equal to its parts, and all the parts equal to the whole: and yet Sir Isaac Newton, (shame on him!) what work has he made, what a building he has erected upon the foundation of this nursery-learning? As to religion, there never was a religion, there never will be one, whether true or false, publickly owned in any country, but children have heard, and ever will hear, more or less of it from those who are placed about them. And if this is, and ever must be the case, whether the religion be true or false; 'tis highly absurd to lay stress on this observation, when the question is about the truth of any religion; for the observation is indifferent to both sides of the question.

We are now, I think, got through the common-place learning, which must forever, it seems, attend upon questions of this nature; and are coming to the very merits of the cause.

And here the Gentleman on the other side thought proper to begin with an account of the people of the Jews, the people in whose country the fact is laid, and who were originally, and in some respects principally concerned in its consequences.

They were, he says, a weak superstitious people, and lived under certain pretended prophecies and predictions; that upon this ground they had, some time before the appearance of Christ Jesus, conceived great expectation of the coming of a victorious prince, who should deliver them from the Roman yoke, and make them all kings and princes. He goes on then to observe, how liable the people were, in this state of things, to be imposed on, and led into rebellion, by any one who was bold enough to take upon him to personate the prince expected. He observes further, that in fact many such imposters did arise, and deceived multitudes to their ruin and destruction.

I have laid these things together, because I do not intend to dispute these matters with the Gentleman. Whether the Jews were a weak and superstitious people, and influenced by false prophecies, or whether they had true prophecies among them, is not material to the present question: it is enough for the Gentleman's argument if I allow the fact to be as he has stated it, that they did expect a victorious prince; that they were upon this account exposed to be practised on by pretenders; and in fact were often so deluded.

This foundation being laid, it was natural to expect, and I believe your Lordship and every one present did expect, that the Gentleman would go on to shew, that Jesus laid hold of this opportunity, struck in with the opinion of the people, and professed himself to be the prince who was to work their deliverance. But so far, it seems, is this from being the case, that the charge upon Jesus is, that he took the contrary part, and set up in opposition to all the popular notions and prejudices of his country; that he interpreted the prophecies to another sense and meaning than his countrymen did; and by his expositions took away all hopes of their ever seeing the victorious deliverer so much wanted and expected.

I know not how to bring the Gentleman's premises and his conclusion to any agreement; they seem to be at a great variance at present. If it be the likeliest method for an imposter to succeed, to build on the popular opinions, prejudices and prophecies of the people; then surely an imposter cannot possibly take a worse method, than to set up in opposition to all the prejudices and prophecies of the country. Where was the art and cunning then of taking this method? Could anything be expected from it but hatred, contempt, and persecution? And did Christ in fact meet with any other treatment from the Jews? And yet when he found, as the Gentleman allows he did, that he must perish in this attempt, did he change his note? did he come about, and drop any intimations agreeable to the notions of the people? It is not pretended. This, which, in any other case which ever happened, would be taken to be a plain mark of great honesty, or great stupidity, or of both, is in the present case art, policy, and contrivance.

But, it seems, Jesus dared not set up to be the victorious prince expected, for victories are not to be counterfeited. I hope it was no crime in him that he did not assume this false character, and try to abuse the credibility of the people; if he had done so, it certainly would have been a crime; and therefore in this point at least he is innocent. I do not suppose the Gentleman imagines the Jews were well founded in their expectation of a temporal prince: and therefore when Christ opposed this conceit at the manifest hazard of his life, as he certainly had truth on his side, so the presumption is, that it was for the sake of truth that he exposed himself.

No. He wanted, we are told, the common and necessary foundation for a new revelation, the authority of an old one to build on. Very well. I will not inquire how common, or how necessary this foundation is to a new revelation; for, be that case as it will, it is evident, that in the method Christ took, he had not, nor could have the supposed advantage of such foundation. For why is this foundation necessary? A friend of the Gentleman's shall tell you "Because it must be difficult, if not impossible, to introduce among men (who in all civilized countries are bred up in the belief of some revealed religion) a revealed religion wholly new, or such as has no reference to a preceding one; for that would be to combat all men on too many respects, and not to proceed on a sufficient number of principles necessary to be assented to by those on whom the first impressions of a new religion are proposed to be made." You see now the reason of the necessity of this foundation: it is, that the new teacher may have the advantage of old popular opinions, and fix himself upon the prejudices of the people. Had Christ any such advantages? or did he seek any such? The people expected a victorious prince; he told them they were mistaken: they held as sacred the traditions of the elders; he told them those traditions made the law of God of none effect: they valued themselves for being the peculiar people of God; he told them, that people from all quarters of the world should be the people of God, and sit down with Abraham, Isaac, and Jacob, in the kingdom: they thought God could be worshipped only at Jerusalem; he told them God might and should be worshipped everywhere: they were superstitious in the observance of the sabbath; he, according to their reckoning, broke it frequently: in a word, their washings of hands and pots, their superstitious distinctions of meats, their prayers in publick, their villanies in secret, were all reproved, exposed, and condemned by him; and the cry ran strongly against him, that he came to destroy the Law and the Prophets. And now, Sir, what advantage did Christ have of your common and necessary foundation? What sufficient number of principles owned by the people did he build on? If he adhered to the old revelation in the true sense, or (which is sufficient to the present argument) in a sense not received by the people, it was in truth the greatest difficulty he had to struggle with: and therefore what could tempt him, but purely a regard for truth, to take upon himself so many difficulties, which might have been avoided, could he have been but silent as to the old revelation, and left the people to their imaginations?

To carry on this plot, we are told, that the next thing which Jesus did, was, to make choice of proper persons to be his disciples. The Gentleman has given us their character; but, as I suppose he has more employment for them before he has done, I desire to defer the consideration of their abilities and conduct till I hear what work he has for them to do. I would only observe, that thus far this plot differs from all that ever I heard of. Imposters generally take advantage of the prejudices of the people, generally too they make choice of cunning dextrous fellows to manage under them; but in this case Jesus opposed all the notions of the people, and made choice of simpletons, it seems, to conduct his contrivances.

But what design, what real end was carrying on all this while? Why, the Gentleman tells us, that the very thing disclaimed, the temporal kingdom, was the real thing aimed at under this disguise. He told the people there was no foundation to expect a temporal deliverer, warned them against all who would set up those pretensions; he declared there was no ground from the ancient prophecies to expect such a prince: and yet by these very means he was working his way to an opportunity of declaring himself to be the very prince the people wanted. We are still upon the marvelous; every step opens new wonders. I blame not the Gentleman; for what but this can be imagined to give any account of these measures imputed to Christ? Be this never so unlikely, yet this is the only thing that can be said. Had Christ been charged with enthusiasm, it would not have been necessary to assign a reason for his conduct: madness is unaccountable: Ratione modoque tractari non vult. But when design, cunning, and fraud are made the charge, and carried to such an height, as to suppose him to be a party to the contrivance of a sham resurrection for himself, it is necessary to say to what end this cunning tended. It was, we are told, to a kingdom: and indeed the temptation was little enough, considering that the chief conductor of the plot was crucified for his pains. But were the means made use of at all probable to achieve the end? Yes, says the Gentleman, that can't be disputed; for they had really this effect, the people would have made him King. Very well: Why was he not King then? Why, it happened unluckily that he would not accept the offer, but withdrew himself from the multitude, and lay concealed until they were dispersed. It will be said, perhaps, that Jesus was a better judge of affairs than the people, and saw that it was not yet time to accept the offer. Be it so; let us see then what follows.

The government was alarmed, and Jesus was looked on as a person dangerous to the state; and he had discernment enough to see that his death was determined and inevitable. What does he do then? Why, to make the best of a bad case, and to save the benefit of his undertaking to those who were to succeed him, he pretends to prophecy of his death, which he knew could not be avoided: Men do not use to play tricks in articulo mortis; but this plot had nothing common, nothing in the ordinary way. But what if it should appear, that after the foretelling of his death (through despair of his fortunes it is said) he had it in his power to set up for King once more, and once more refused the opportunity? Men in despair lay hold on the least help, and never refuse the greatest. Now, the case was really so. After he had foretold his crucifixion, he came to Jerusalem in the triumphant manner the Gentleman mentioned; the people strewed his way with boughs and flowers, and were all at his devotion; the Jewish governors lay still for fear of the people. Why was not this opportunity laid hold on to seize the kingdom, or at least to secure himself from the ignominious death he expected? For whose sake was he contented to die? for whose sake did he contrive this plot of his resurrection? Wife and children he had none; his nearest relations gave little credit to him; his disciples were not fit even to be trusted with the secret, nor capable to manage any advantage that could arise from it. However, the Gentleman tells us, a kingdom has arisen out of this plot, a kingdom of priests. But when did it arise? Some hundred years after the death of Christ, in opposition to his will, and almost to the subversion of his religion. And yet we are told this kingdom was the thing he had in view. I am apt to think the Gentleman is persuaded, that the dominion he complains of is contrary to the spirit of the gospel; I am sure some of his friends have taken great pains to prove it is so. How then can it be charged as the intention of the gospel to introduce it? Whatever the case was, it cannot surely be suspected that Christ died to make Popes and Cardinals. The alterations which have happened in the doctrines and practices of churches, since the Christian religion was settled by those who had an authentick commission to settle it, are quite out of the question, when the inquiry is about the truth of the Christian religion. Christ and his Apostles did not vouch for the truth of all that should be taught in the church in future times; nay, they foretold and fore warned the world against such corrupt teachers. It is therefore absurd to challenge the religion of Christ, because of the corruptions which have spread among Christians. The gospel has no more concern with them, and ought no more to be charged with them, than with the doctrines of the Alcoran.

There is but one observation more, I think, which the Gentleman made under this head. Jesus, he says, referred to the authority of ancient prophecies to prove that the Messias was to die and rise again; the ancient books referred to are extant, and no such prophecies, he says, are to be found. Now, whether the Gentleman can find these prophecies or no, is not material to the present question. It is allowed that Christ foretold his own death and resurrection; if the resurrection was managed by fraud, Christ was certainly in the fraud himself, by foretelling the fraud which was to happen: disprove therefore the resurrection, and we shall have no further occasion for prophecy. On the other side, by foretelling the resurrection, he certainly put the proof of his mission on the truth of the event. Whether it be the character of the Messias, in the ancient Prophets, or no, that he should die, and rise again; without doubt Jesus is not the Messias, if he did not rise again: for, by his own prophecy, he made it part of the character of the Messias. If the event justified the prediction, it is such an evidence as no man of sense and reason can reject. One would naturally think, that the foretelling his resurrection, and giving such publick notice to expect it, that his keenest enemies were fully apprised of it, carried with it the greatest mark of sincere dealing. It stands thus far clear of the suspicion of fraud. And had it proceeded from enthusiasm, and an heated imagination, the dead body at least would have rested in the grave, and without further evidence have confuted such pretensions: and since the dead body was not only carried openly to the grave, but there watched and guarded, and yet could never afterwards be found, never heard of more as a dead body, there must of necessity have been either a real miracle, or a great fraud in this case. Enthusiasm dies with the man, and has no operation on his dead body. There is therefore here no medium: you must either admit the miracle, or prove the fraud.

Judge. Mr. A. You are at liberty either to reply to what has been said under this head, or to go on with your cause

Mr. A. My Lord, the observations I laid before you, were but introductory to the main evidences on which the merits of the cause must rest. The Gentleman concluded, that here must be a real miracle or a great fraud; a fraud, he means, to which Jesus in his lifetime was a party. There is, he says, no medium. I beg his pardon. Why might it not be an enthusiasm in the master which occasioned the prediction, and fraud in the servants who put it in execution?

Mr. B. My Lord, This is new matter, and not a reply. The Gentleman opened this transaction as a fraud from one end to the other. Now he supposes Christ to have been an honest, poor enthusiast, and the disciples only to be cheats.

Judge. Sir, if you go to new matter, the council on the other side must be admitted to answer.

Mr. A. My Lord, I have no such intention. I was observing, that the account I gave of Jesus was only to introduce the evidence that is to be laid before the court. It cannot be expected, that I should know all the secret designs of this contrivance, especially considering that we have but short accounts of this affair, and those too conveyed through hands of friends and parties to the plot. In such a case it is enough if we can imagine what the views probably were; and in such case too it must be very easy for a Gentleman of parts to raise contrary imaginations, and to argue plausibly from them. But the Gentleman has rightly observed, that if the resurrection be a fraud, there is an end to all pretensions, good or bad, that were to be supported by it: therefore I shall go on to prove this fraud, which is one main part of the cause now to be determined.

I beg leave to remind you, that Jesus in his lifetime foretold his death, and that he should rise again the third day. The first part of his prediction was accomplished: he died on the cross and was buried. I will not trouble you with the particulars of his crucifixion, death, and burial; it is a well known story.

Mr. B. My Lord, I desire to know, whether the Gentleman charges any fraud upon this part of the history. Perhaps he may be of the opinion by and by, that there was a sleight of hand in the crucifixion, and that Christ only counterfeited death.

Mr. A. No, no; have no such fears; he was not crucified by his disciples; but by the Romans and the Jews; and they were in very good earnest. I will prove beyond contradiction, that the dead body was fairly laid in the tomb; and it will be well for you if you can get it as fairly out again.

Judge. Go on with your evidence.

Mr. A. My Lord, the crucifixion being over, the dead body was conveyed to a sepulchre; and in the general opinion there seemed to be an end of the whole design. But the governors of the Jews, watchful for the safety of the people, called to mind that Jesus in his lifetime had said, that he would rise again on the third day. It may at first sight seem strange that they should give any attention to such a prophecy; a prophecy big with confidence and presumption, and which to the common sense of mankind carried its confutation along with it: and "there is no other nation in the world which would not have slighted such a vain prognostication of a known imposter." But they had warning to be watchful. It was not long before, that the people "had like to have been fatally deluded and imposed on by him in the pretended resuscitation of Lazarus." They had fully discovered the cheat in the case of Lazarus, and had narrowly escaped the dangerous consequences of it. And though Jesus was dead, yet he had many disciples and followers alive, who were ready enough to combine in any fraud, to verify the prediction of their master. Should they succeed, the rulers foresaw, the consequences in this case would be more fatal than those which before they had narrowly escaped. Upon this account they addressed themselves to the Roman governor, told him how the case was, and desired that he would grant them a guard to watch the sepulchre; that the service would not be long, for the prediction limited the resurrection to the third day; and when that was over, the soldiers might be released from the duty. Pilate granted the request; and a guard was set to watch the sepulchre.

This was not all. The chief priests took another method to prevent all frauds, and it was the best that could possibly be taken; which was, to seal up the door of the sepulchre. To understand to what purpose this caution was used, you need only consider what is intended by sealing up doors, and boxes, or writings. Is it not for the satisfaction of all parties concerned, that they may be sure things are in the state they left them, when they come and find their seals not injured? This was the method used by Darius, when Daniel was cast into the lions den; he sealed the door of the den. And for what purpose? Was it not to satisfy himself and his court, that no art had been used to preserve Daniel? And when he came and saw Daniel safe, and his seal untouched, he was satisfied. And indeed if we consider the thing rightly, a seal thus used imports a covenant. If you deliver writings to a person sealed, and he accepts them so, your delivery and his acceptance implies a covenant between you, that the writings shall be delivered and the seal whole; and should the seal be broken, it would be a manifest fraud, and breach of trust. Nay, so strongly is this covenant implied, that there needs no special agreement in the case; it is a compact which men are put under by the law of nations, and the common consent of mankind. When you send a letter sealed to the post- house, you have not indeed a special agreement with all persons through whose hands it passes, that it shall not be opened by any hand , but his only to whom it is directed; yet men know themselves to be under this restraint, and that it is unlawful and dishonorable to transgress it.

Since then the sepulchre was sealed; since the seal imported a covenant, consider who were the parties to this covenant. They could be no other than the chief priests on one side, and the apostles on the other. To prove this, no special agreement need be shewn. On one side, there was a concern to see the prophecy fulfilled; on the other, to prevent fraud in fulfilling it. The sum of their agreement was naturally this, that the seals should be opened at the time appointed for the resurrection, that all parties might see and be satisfied, whether the dead body was come to life or no.

What now would any reasonable man expect from these circumstances? Don't you expect to hear, that the chief priests and the apostles met at the time appointed, opened the seals, and that the matter in dispute was settled beyond all controversy one way or other? But see how it happened, The seals were broken, the body stolen away in the night by the disciples; none of the chief priests present, or summoned to see the seals opened. The guards, when examined, were forced to confess the truth, though joined with an acknowledgement of their guilt; which made them liable to be punished by Pilate: they confessed that they were asleep, and in the mean time that the body was stolen away by the disciples.

This evidence of the Roman soldiers, and the far stronger evidence arising from the clandestine method of breaking up the seals, are sufficient proofs of fraud.

But there is another circumstance in the case, of equal weight. Though the seals did not prevent the cheat entirely, yet they effectually falsified the prediction. According to the prediction, Jesus was to rise on the third day, or after the third day. At this time the chief priests intended to be present, and probably would have been attended by a great multitude. This made it impossible to play any tricks at that time; and therefore the apostles were forced the hasten the plot: and accordingly the resurrection happened a day before its time; for the body was buried on the Friday, and was gone early in the morning on Sunday.

These are plain facts; facts drawn from the accounts given to us by those who are friends to the belief of the resurrection. The Gentleman won't call these imaginations, or complain that I have given him schemes instead of evidence.

Mr. B. My Lord, I am now to consider that part of the argument upon which the Gentleman lays the greatest stress. He has given us his evidence; mere evidence, he says, unmixed, and clear of all schemes and imaginations. In one thing indeed he has been as good as his word; he has proved beyond contradiction, that Christ died, and was laid in the sepulchre: for, without doubt, when the Jews sealed the stone, they took care to see that the body was there; otherwise their precaution was useless. He has proved too, that the prediction of Christ concerning his own resurrection, was a thing publickly known in all Jerusalem; for he owns, that this gave occasion for all the care that was taken to prevent fraud. If this open prediction implies a fraudulent design, the evidence is strong with the Gentleman: but if it shall appear to be, what it really was, the greatest mark that could be given of sincerity and plain dealing in the whole affair, the evidence will still be as strong, but the weight of it will fall on the wrong side for the Gentleman's purpose.

In the next place, the Gentleman seems to be at a great loss to account for the credit which the chief priests gave to the prediction of the resurrection, by the care they took to prevent it. He thinks the thing in itself was too extravagant and absurd to deserve any regard; and that no one would have regarded such a prediction in any other time or place. I agree with the Gentleman entirely: but then I demand of him a reason why the chief priests were under any concern about this prediction. Was it because they had plainly discovered him to be a cheat and an imposter? It is impossible. This reason would have convinced them of the folly and presumption of the prediction. It must therefore necessarily be, that they had discovered something in the life and actions of Christ which raised this jealousy, and made them listen to a prophecy in his case, which in any other case they would have despised. And what could this be, but the secret conviction they were under, by his many miracles, of his extraordinary powers? This care therefore of the chief priests over his dead, helpless body, is a lasting testimony of the mighty works which Jesus did in his lifetime; for had the Jews been persuaded that he performed no wonders in his life, I think they would not have been afraid of seeing any done by him after his death.

But the Gentleman is of another mind. He says, they had discovered a plain cheat in the case of Lazarus, whom Christ had pretended to raise from the dead; and therefore they took all this care to guard against a like cheat.

I begin now to want evidence; I am forbid to call this imagination, what else to call it I know not. There is not the least intimation given from history, that there was any cheat in the case of Lazarus, or that any one suspected a cheat. Lazarus lived in the country after he was raised from the dead; and though his life was secretly and basely sought after, yet no body had the courage to call to a trial for his part in the cheat. It may be said, perhaps, the rulers were terrified. Very well: but they were not terrified when they had Christ in their possession, when they brought him to a trial; why did they not then object this cheat to Christ? It would have been much to their purpose. Instead of that, they accuse him of a design to pull down their temple, to destroy their law, and of blasphemy; but not one word of any fraud in the case of Lazarus, or any other case.

But not to enter into the merits of this cause, which has in it too many circumstances for your present consideration; let us take the case to be as the Gentleman states it, that the cheat in the case of Lazarus was detected; what consequence is to be expected? In all other cases, impostors, once discovered, grow odious and contemptible, and quite incapable of doing further mischief; so little are they regarded, that even when they tell the truth, they are neglected. Was it so in this case? No, says the Gentleman; the Jews were the more careful that Christ should not cheat them in his own resurrection. Surely this is a most singular case. When the people thought him a Prophet, the chief priests sought to kill him, and thought his death would put an end to his pretensions: when they and the people had discovered him to be a cheat, then they thought him not safe, even when he was dead, but were afraid he should prove a true Prophet, and, according to his own prediction, rise again. A needless, a preposterous fear!

In the next place, the Gentleman tells us how proper the care was that the chief priests took. I agree perfectly with him. Human policy could not invent a more proper method to guard against and prevent all fraud. They delivered the sepulchre, with the dead body in it, to a company of Roman soldiers, who had orders from their officer to watch the sepulchre. Their care went further still; they sealed the door of the sepulchre.

Upon this occasion, the Gentleman has explained the use of seals when applied to such purposes. They imply, he says, a covenant, that the things sealed up shall remain in the condition they are till the parties to the sealing agree to open them. I see no reason to enter into the learning about seals: let it be as the Gentleman has opened it; what then?

Why then, it seems, the apostles and chief priests were in a covenant that there should be no resurrection, at least no opening of the door, till they met together at an appointed time to view and unseal the door.

Your Lordship and the court will now consider the probability of this supposition. When Christ was seized and carried to his trial, his disciples fled, out of a just apprehension that they should, if apprehended, be sacrificed with their master. Peter indeed followed him; but his courage soon failed, and it is well known in what manner he denied him. After the death of Christ, his disciples were so far from being ready to engage for his resurrection, or to enter into terms and agreements for the manner in which it should be done, that they themselves did not believe it ever would be; they gave over all hopes and thoughts of it; and far from entering into engagements with the chief priests, their whole concern was, to keep themselves concealed from them. This is a well known case, and I will not trouble you with particular authorities to prove this truth. Can any man now in his right senses think, that the disciples under these circumstances entered into this covenant with the Jews? I believe the Gentleman don't think it, and for that reason says, that seals so used import a covenant without a special agreement. Be it so; and it must then be allowed, that the apostles were no more concerned in these seals, than every other man in the country, and no more answerable for them; for the covenant reached to every body as well as to them, since they were under no special contract.

But I beg pardon for spending your time unnecessarily, when the simple plain account of this matter will best answer all these jealousies and suspicions. The Jews, it is plain, were exceedingly solicitous about this event; for this reason they obtained a guard from Pilate; and when they had, they were still suspicious lest their guards should deceive them, and enter into combination against them. To secure this point, they sealed the door, and required of the guards to deliver up the sepulchre to them sealed as it was. This is the natural and true account of the matter. Do but consider it in a parallel case. Suppose a prince should set a guard at the door of his treasury, and the officer who placed the guard should seal the door, and say to the soldiers, You shall be answerable for the seal if I find it broken: would not all the world understand the seal to be fixed to guard against the soldiers, who might, though employed to keep off others, be ready enough to pilfer themselves? This is in all such cases but a necessary care; you may place guards, and when you do all is in their power: Et quis custodes custodiat ipsos?

But it seems, that, notwithstanding all this care, the seals were broken, and the body gone. If you complain of this, Sir, demand satisfaction of your guards; they only are responsible for it: the disciples had no more to do in it than you or I.

The guards, the Gentleman says, have confessed the truth, and owned that they were asleep, and that the disciples in the mean time stole away the body. I wish the guards were in court, I would ask them, how they came to be so punctual in relating what happened when they were asleep? what induced them to believe that the body was stolen at all? what, that it was stolen by the disciples; since by their own confession they were asleep and say nothing, saw no body? But since they are not to be had, I would desire to ask the Gentleman the same questions; and whether he has any authorities in point, to shew, that ever any man was admitted as an evidence in any court, to prove a fact which happened when he was asleep? I see the Gentleman is uneasy; I'll press the matter no further.

As this story has no evidence to support it, so neither has it any probability. The Gentleman has given you the character of the disciples; that they were weak, ignorant men, full of the popular prejudices and superstitions of their country,which stuck close to them notwithstanding their long acquaintance with their master. The apostles are not much wronged in this account; and is it likely that such men should engage in so desperate design, as to steal away the body, in opposition to the combined power of the Jews and Romans? What could tempt them to it? What good could the dead body do them? Or if it could have done them any, what hope had they to succeed in their attempt? A dead body is not to be removed by sleight of hand; it requires many hands to move it: besides, the great stone at the mouth of the sepulchre was to be removed; which could not be done silently, or by men walking on tip-toes to prevent discovery: so that if the guards had really been asleep, yet there was no encouragement to go on this enterprise; for it is hardly possible to suppose, but that rolling away the stone, moving the body, the hurry and confusion of carrying it off, must awaken them.

But supposing the thing was practicable, yet the attempt was such as the disciples consistently with their own notions could not undertake. The Gentleman says, they continued all their master's lifetime to expect to see him a temporal prince; and a friend of the Gentleman's has observed, what is equally true, that they had the same expectation after his death. Consider now their case. Their master was dead; and they are to contrive to steal away his body. For what? Did they expect to make a King of the dead body, if they could get it into their power? Or did they think, if they had it, they could raise it to life again? If they trusted so far to their master's prediction, as to expect his resurrection, (which I think is evident they did not), could they yet think the resurrection depended on their having the dead body? It is in all views absurd. But the Gentleman supposes, that they meant to carry on the design for themselves, in the master's, if they could but have persuaded the people to believe him risen from the dead. But he does not consider, that by this supposition he strips the disciples of every part of their character at once, and presents to us a new set of men, in every respect different from the former. The former disciples were weak, plain men; but these are bold, hardy, cunning, and contriving: the former were full of the superstitions of their country, and expected a prince from the authority of their Prophets; but these were despisers of the Prophets, and of the notions of their countrymen, and are designing to turn these fables to their own advantage; for it cannot be supposed that they believed the Prophets, and at the same time thought to accomplish or defeat them by so manifest a cheat, to which they themselves at least were conscious.

But let us take leave of these suppositions, and see how the true evidence is this case stands. Guards were placed, and they did their duty. But what are guards and sentinels against the power of God? An angel of the Lord opened the sepulchre; the guards saw him, and became like dead men. This account they gave to the chief priests, who, still persisting in their obstinacy, bribed the guards to tell the contradictory story, of their being asleep, and the body stolen.

I cannot but observe to your Lordship, that all these circumstances, so much questioned and suspected, were necessary circumstances, supposing the resurrection to be true. The seal was broken, the body came out of the sepulchre, the guards were placed in vain to prevent it. Be it so: I desire to know, whether the Gentleman thinks that the seal put God under covenant? or could prescribe to him a method for performing this great work? or whether he thinks the guards were placed to maintain the seal in opposition to the power of God? If he will maintain neither of these points, then the opening of the seals, notwithstanding the guard set upon them, will be an evidence, not of the fraud, but of the power of the resurrection; and the guards will have nothing to answer for, but only this, that they were not stronger than God. The seal was a proper check upon the guards: the Jews had no other meaning in it; they could not be so stupid as to imagine, that they could by this contrivance disappoint the designs of providence. And it is surprising to hear these circumstances made use of to prove the resurrection to be a fraud, which yet could not but happen, supposing the resurrection to be true.

But there is another circumstance still, which the Gentleman reckons very material, and upon which I find great stress is laid. The resurrection happened, we are told, a day sooner than the prediction imported. The reason assigned for it is, that the execution of the plot at the time appointed was rendered impracticable, because the chief priests, an probably great numbers of the people, were prepared to visit the sepulchre at that time; and therefore the disciples were under a necessity of hastening their plot.

This observation is entirely inconsistent with the supposition upon which the reasoning stands. The Gentleman has all along supposed the resurrection to have been managed by fraud, and not by violence. And indeed violence, if there had been an opportunity of using it, would have been insignificant: beating the guards, and removing the dead body by force, would have destroyed all pretences to a resurrection. Now, surely the guards, supposing them to be enough in number to withstand all violence, were at least sufficient to prevent or to discover fraud. What occasion then to hasten the plot for fear of numbers meeting at the tomb, since there were numbers always present sufficient to discover any fraud; the only method that could be used in the case?

Suppose then that we could not give a satisfactory account of the way of reckoning the time from the crucifixion to the resurrection; yet this we can say, that the resurrection happened during the time that the guards had the sepulchre in keeping; and it is impossible to imagine what opportunity this could give to fraud. Had the time been delayed, the guards removed, and then a resurrection pretended, it might with some colour of reason have been said, Why did he not come within his time? why did he chuse to come after his time, when all witnesses, who had patiently expected the appointed hour, were withdrawn? But now what is to be objected? You think he came too soon. But were not your guards at the door when he came? did they not see what happened? and what other satisfaction could you have had, supposing he had come a day later?

By saying of this, I do not mean the decline the Gentleman's objection, which is founded upon a mistake of a way of speaking, common to the Jews and other people; who, when they name any number of days and years, include the first and last of the days or years to make up the sum. Christ, alluding to his own resurrection, says, In three days I will raise it up. The angels report his prediction thus, The Son of Man shall be crucified, and the third day rise again. Elsewhere it is said, After three days; and again, that he was to be in the bowels of the earth three days and three nights. These expressions are equivalent to each other; for we always reckon the night into the day, when we reckon by so many days. If you agree to do a thing ten days hence, you stipulate for forbearance for the nights as well as days; and therefore, in reckoning, two days, and two days and two nights, are the same thing. That the expression, After three days, means inclusive days, is proved by Grotius on Matt. xxvii. 63 and by others. The prediction therefore was, that he would rise on the third day. Now, he was crucified on Friday and buried; he lay in the grave all Saturday, and rose early on Sunday morning. But the Gentleman thinks he ought not to have risen before Monday. Pray try what the use of common language requires to be understood in a like case. Suppose you were told, that your friend sickened on Friday, was let blood on Saturday, and the third day he died; what day would you think he died on? If you have any doubt about it, put the question to the first plain man you meet, and he will resolve it. The Jews could have no doubt in this case; for so they practised in one of the highest points of their law. Every male child was to be circumcised on the eighth day. How did they reckon the days? Why, the day of the birth was one, and the day of the circumcision another; and though a child was born towards the every end of the first day, he was capable of circumcision on any time of the eighth day. And therefore it is not new nor strange, that the third day, in our case, should be reckoned into the number, though Christ rose at the very beginning of it. It is more strange to reckon whole years in this manner; and yet this is the constant method observed in Ptolemy's canon, the most valuable piece of ancient chronology, next to the Bible, now extant. If a King lived over the first day of a year, and died the week after, that whole year is reckoned to his reign.

I have now gone through the several objections upon this head: what credit they may gain in this age, I know not; but 'tis plain they had no credit when they were first spread abroad; nay, 'tis evident, that the very persons who set abroad this story of the body being stolen, did not believe it themselves. And, not to insist here upon the plain fact, which was, that the guards were hired to tell this lie by the chief priests, it will appear from the after conduct of the chief priests themselves, that they were conscious that the story was false. Not long after the resurrection of Christ, the disciples having received new power from above, appeard publickly in Jerusalem, and in the very temple, and testified the resurrection of Christ, even before those who had murdered him. What now do the chief priests do? They seize upon the apostles, they threaten them, they beat them,. they scourge them, and all to stop their mouths, insisting that they should say no more of the matter. But why did they not, when they had the disciples in their power, charge them directly with their notorious cheat in stealing the body, and expose them to the people as imposters? This had been much more to their purpose, than all their menaces and ill usage, and would more effectually have undeceived the people. But of this not one word is said. They try to murder them, enter into combinations to assassinate them, prevail with Herod to put one of them to death; but not so much as a charge against them of any fraud in the resurrection. Their orator Tertullus, who could not have missed so fine a topick of declamation, had there been but a suspicion to support it, is quite silent on this head, and is content to flourish on the common-place of sedition and heresy, profaning the temple, and the like: very trifles to his cause, in comparison to the other accusation, had there been any ground to make use of it. And yet as it happens, we are sure the very question of the resurrection came under debate; for Festus tells King Agrippa, that the Jews had certain questions against Paul, of one Jesus which was dead, whom Paul affirmed to be alive. After this, Agrippa hears Paul himself; and had he suspected, much less had he been convinced that there was a cheat in the resurrection, he would hardly have said to Paul at the end of the conference, Almost thou persuadest me to be a Christian.

But let us see what the council and senate of the children of Israel thought of this matter, in the most solemn and serious deliberation they ever had about it. Not long after the resurrection, the apostles were taken; the High Priest thought the matter of that weight, that he summoned the council and senate of the children of Israel. The apostles are brought before them, and make their defence. Part of their defence is in these words: The God of our fathers raised up Jesus, whom ye slew and hanged on a tree. The defence was indeed a heavy charge upon the senate, and in the warmth of their anger, their first resolution was to slay them all. But Gamaliel, one of the council, stood up, and told them, that the matter deserved more consideration. He recounted to them the history of several imposters who had perished, and concluded with respect to the case of the apostles then before them: If this work be of men, it will come to nought; but if it be of God, ye cannot overthrow it, lest haply ye be found to fight against God. The council agreed to this advice, and after some ill treatment, the apostles were discharged. I ask now, and let any man of common sense answer, Could Gamaliel possibly have given this advice, and supposed that the hand of God might be with the apostles, if he had known that there was a cheat discovered in the resurrection of Jesus? Could the whole senate have followed this advice, had they believed the discovery of the cheat? Was there not among them one man wise enough to say, How can you suppose God to have anything to do in this affair, when the resurrection of Jesus, upon which all depends, was a notorious cheat, and manifestly proved to be so? I should but lessen the weight of this authority by saying more, and therefore I will rest here, and give way to the Gentleman to go on with his accusation.

Mr. A. My Lord, Before I proceed any further, I beg leave to say a few words in reply to what the Gentleman has offered on this head.

The Gentleman thinks, that the detection in the case of Lazarus ought to have made the Jews quite unconcerned in the case of Jesus, and secure as to the event of his own resurrection. He says very true, supposing their care had been for themselves: but governors have another care upon their hands, the care of their people; and 'tis not enough for them to guard against being imposed on themselves, they must be watchful to guard the multitude against frauds and deceits. The chief priests were satisfied indeed of the fraud in the case of Lazarus, yet they saw the people deceived by it; and for this reason, and not for their own satisfaction, they used the caution in the case of the resurrection of Jesus, which I before laid before you. In so doing, they are well justified; and the inconsistency charged on the other side, between their opinion of Jesus, and their fear of being imposed on by his pretended resurrection, is fully answered.

The next observation relates to the seal of the sepulchre. The Gentleman thinks the seal was used as a check upon the Roman soldiers. But what reason had the Jews to suspect them? They were not disciples of Jesus; they were servants of the Roman governor, and employed in the service of the Jews: and I leave it to the court to judge, whether the Jews set the seal to guard against their friends, or their enemies? But if the seals were really used against the guards, then the breaking of the seals is a proof that the guards were corrupted: and if so, 'tis easy to conceive how the body was removed.

As to the disciples, the Gentleman observes, that the part allotted them in the management of the resurrection supposes an unaccountable change in their character. It will not be long before the Gentleman will have occasion for as great a change in their character: for these weak men you will find soon employed in converting the world, and sent to appear before Kings and Princes in the name of their master; soon you will see them grow wise and powerful, and every way qualified for their extensive and important business. The only difference between me and the Gentleman on the other side will be found to be this, that I date this change a little earlier than he does: A small matter, surely, to determine the right of this controversy.

The last observation relates to King Agrippa's complaisance to Paul, and Gamaliel's advice. I cannot answer for Agrippa's meaning: but certainly he meant but little; and if this matter is to be tried by his opinion, we know that he never did turn Christian. As for Gamaliel, 'tis probable that he saw great numbers of the people engaged zealously in favour of the apostles, and might think it prudent to pass the matter over in silence, and not to come to extremities. This is a common case in all governments: the multitude and their leaders often escape punishment, not because they do not deserve it, but because it is not, in some circumstances, prudent to exact it.

I pass over these things lightly, because the next article contains the great, to us indeed, who live at this distance, the only great question; for whatever reason the Jews had to believe the resurrection, it is nothing to us, unless the story has been conveyed to us upon such evidence as is sufficient to support the weight laid on it.

My Lord, we are now to enter upon the last and main article of this case; the nature of the evidence upon which the credit of the resurrection stands. Before I inquire into the qualifications of the particular witnesses whose words we are desired to take in this case, I would ask, why this evidence, which manifestly relates to the most essential point of Christianity, was not put beyond all exception? Many of the miracles of Christ are said to be done in the streets, nay even in the temple, under the observation of all the world; but the like is not so much as pretended as to this; nay, we have it upon the confession of Peter, the ringleader of the apostles, that Christ appeared, not to all the people, but unto witnesses chosen before of God. Why picking and culling of witnesses in this case more than in any other? Does it not import some suspicion, raise some jealousy, that this case would not bear the publick light?

I would ask more particularly, Why did not Jesus after his resurrection appear openly to the chief priests and rulers of the Jews? Since his commission related to them in an especial manner, why were not his credentials laid before them? The resurrection is acknowledged to be the chief proof of his mission, why then was it concealed from those who were more than all others concerned in the event of his mission? Suppose an ambassador from some foreign prince should come into England, make his publick entry through the city, pay and receive visits, and at last refuse to shew any letters of credence, or to wait on the King, what would you think of him? Whatever you would think in that case, you must think in this; for there is no difference between them.

But we must take the evidence as it is. It was thought proper, in this case, to have select chosen witnesses; and we must now consider who they were, and what reason we have to take their word.

The first witness was an angel, or angels. They appeared like men to some women who went early to the sepulchre. If they appeared like men, upon what ground are we to take them for angels? The women saw men, and therefore they can witness only to the seeing of men. But I suppose it is the women's judgement, and not their evidence, that we are to follow in this case. Here then we have a story of one apparition to support the credit of another apparition: and the first apparition hath not so much as the evidence of the women to support it, but is grounded on their superstition, ignorance, and fear. Every country can afford an hundred instances of this kind; and there is this common to them all, that as learning and common sense prevail in any country, they die away, and are no more heard of.

The next witnesses are the women themselves. The wisest men can hardly guard themselves against the fears of superstition; poor silly women therefore in this case must needs be unexceptionable witnesses, and fit to be admitted into the number of the chosen witnesses to attest this fact. One part of the account given of them is very rational, that they were surprised and frightened beyond measure; and I leave it to your Lordship and the court to judge, how well qualified they were to give a just relation of what passed.

After this, Jesus appears to two of his disciples as they were upon a journey; he joins them, and introduces a discourse about himself; and spent much time, till it began to grow dark, in expounding the prophecies relating to the death and resurrection of the Messias. All this while, the disciples knew him not. But then going into an house to lodge together, at supper he broke bread, and gave it to them; immediately they knew him, immediately he vanished. Here then are two witnesses more. But what will you call them? eye-witnesses? Why their eyes were open, and they had their senses, when he reasoned with them and they knew him not. So far therefore they are witnesses that it was not he. Tell us therefore upon what account you reject the evidence of their sense before the breaking of the bread, and insist on it afterwards? And why did Jesus vanish as soon as known; which has more of the air of an apparition, than of the appearance of a real man restored to life?

Cleopas, who was one of these two disciples, finds out the apostles, to make the report of what had passed to them. No sooner was the story told, but Jesus appears among them. They were all frightened and confounded, and thought they saw a spectre. He rebukes them for infidelity, and their slowness in believing the prophecies of his resurrection: and though he refused before to let the women touch him (a circumstance which I ought not to have omitted); yet now he invites the apostles to handle him, to examine his hands and feet, and search the wounds of the cross. But what body was it they examined? The same that came in when the doors were shut; the same that vanished from the two disciples; the same that the women might not touch: in a word, a body quite different from a human body, which we know cannot pass through walls, or appear or disappear at pleasure. What then could their hands or eyes inform them of in this case? Besides, is it credible that God should raise a body imperfectly, with the very wounds in it of which it died? Or, if the wounds were such as destroyed the body before, how could a natural body subsist with them afterwards?

There are more appearances of Jesus recorded; but so much of the same kind, so liable to the same difficulties and objections, that I will not trouble your Lordship and the court with a distinct enumeration of them. If the Gentleman on the other side finds any advantage in any of them more than in these mentioned, I shall have an opportunity to consider them in my reply. It may seem surprising to you, perhaps, that a matter of this moment was trusted upon such evidence as this: but it will be still more surprising to consider that the several nations who received the gospel, and submitted to the faith of this article, had not even this evidence: for what people or nation had the evidence of the angels, the women or even of all the apostles? So far from it, that every country had its single apostle, and received the faith upon the credit of his single evidence. We have followed our ancestors without inquiry; and if you examine the thing to the bottom, our belief was originally built upon the word of one man. I shall trouble you, Sir, but with one observation more; which is this: That although in common life we act in a thousand instances upon the faith and credit of human testimony; yet the reason for so doing is not the same in the case before us. In common affairs, where nothing is asserted but what is probable, and possible, according to the usual course of nature, a reasonable degree of evidence ought to determine every man: for the very probability, or possibility of the thing, is an support to the evidence; and in such cases we have no doubt but a man's senses qualify him to be a witness. But when the thing testified is contrary to the order of nature, and, at first sight at least, impossible, what evidence can be sufficient to overturn the constant evidence of nature, which she gives us in the uniform and regular method of her operations? If a man tells me he has been in France, I ought to give a reason for not believing him; but if he tells me he comes from the grave what reason can he give why I should believe him? In the case before us, since the body raised from the grave differed from common natural bodies, as we have before seen; how can I be assured that the apostles' senses qualified them to judge at all of this body; whether it was the same, or not the same which was buried? They handled the body, which yet could pass through doors and walls; they saw it, and sometimes knew it, at other times knew it not. In a word, it seems to be a case exempt from human evidence. Men have limited senses, and a limited reason: when they act within their limits, we may give credit to them; but when they talk of things removed beyond the reach of their senses and reason, we must quit our own, if we believe theirs. Mr. B. My Lord, in answering the objections under this head I shall find myself obliged to change the order in which the gentleman thought proper to place them. He began with complaining, that Christ did not appear publickly to the Jews after his resurrection, and especially to the chief priests and rulers; and seemed to argue, as if such evidence would have put the matter in question out of all doubt: but he concluded with an observation to prove that no evidence in this case can be sufficient; that a resurrection is thing in nature impossible, at least impossible to be proved to the satisfaction of a rational inquirer. If this be the case, why does he require more evidence, since none can be sufficient? Or to what purpose is it to vindicate the particular evidence of the resurrection of Christ, so long as this general prejudice, that a resurrection is incapable of being proved, remains unremoved? I am under a necessity therefore to consider this observation in the first place, that it might lie as a dead weight upon all I have to offer in support of the evidence of Christ's resurrection.

The gentleman allows it to be reasonable in many cases to act upon the testimony and credit of others; but he thinks this should be confined to such cases, where the thing testified is probable, possible, and according to the usual course of nature. The Gentleman does not, I suppose, pretend to know the extent of all natural possibilities, much less will he suppose them to be generally known; and therefore his meaning must be, that the testimony of witnesses is to be received only in cases which appear to us to be possible. In any other sense we can have no dispute; for mere impossibilities, which can never exist, can never be proved. Taking the observation therefore in this sense, the proposition is this: That the testimony of others ought not to be admitted, but in such matters as appear probable, or at least possible to our conceptions. For instance: A man who lives in a warm climate, and never saw ice, ought upon no evidence to believe, that rivers freeze, and grow hard, in cold countries; for this is improbable, contrary to the usual course of nature, and impossible according to his notion of things. And yet we all know, that this is a plain manifest case discernible by the senses of men; of which therefore they are qualified to be good witnesses. An hundred such instances might be named; but 'tis needless: for surely nothing is more apparently absurd than to make one man's ability in discerning and his veracity in reporting plain facts, depend upon the skill or ignorance of the hearer. And what has the Gentleman said upon this occasion against the resurrection, more than any man who never saw ice might say against an hundred honest witnesses, who assert that water turns to ice in cold climates?

Yet it is very true, that men do not so easily believe, upon testimony of others, things which to them seem improbable or impossible; but the reason is not, because the thing itself admits no evidence, but because the hearer's preconceived opinion outweighs the credit of the reporter and makes his veracity to be called in question. For instance it is natural for a stone to roll down hill, it is unnatural for it to roll up hill: but a stone moving uphill is as much the object of sense as a stone moving downhill; and all men in their senses are as capable of seeing and judging and reporting the fact in one case, as in the other. Should a man then tell you, that he saw a stone go uphill of its own accord, you might question his veracity; but you could not say the thing admitted no evidence, because it was contrary to the law and usual course of nature; for the law of nature formed to yourself from your own experience and reasoning is quite independent of the matter of fact which the man testifies: and whenever you see facts yourself, which contradict your notions of the law of nature, you admit the facts, because you believe yourself; when you do not admit like facts upon the evidence of others, it is because you do not believe them, and not because the facts in their own nature exclude all evidence.

Suppose a man should tell you, that he was come from the dead, you would be apt to suspect his evidence. But what would you suspect? That he was not alive when you heard him, saw him, felt him, and conversed with him? You could not suspect this, without giving up all your senses and acting in this case as you act in no other. Here then you would question, whether the man had ever been dead? But would you say, that it is incapable of being made plain by human testimony, that this or that man died a year ago? It can't be said. Evidence in this case is admitted in all courts perpetually

Consider it the other way. Suppose you saw a man publicly executed, his body afterwards was wounded by the executioner, and carried and laid in the grave; that after this you should be told, that the man was come to life again; what would you suspect in this case? Not that the man had never been dead; for that you saw yourself: but you would suspect whether he was now alive. But would you say this case excluded all human testimony and that men could not possibly discern , whether one with whom they conversed familiarly was alive or no? Upon what ground could you say this? A man rising from the grave is an object of sense, and can give the same evidence of his being alive, as any other man in the world can give. So that a resurrection considered only as a fact to be proved by evidence, is a plain case; it requires no greater ability in the witnesses, than that they be able to distinguish between a man dead, and a man alive: a point in which I believe every man living thinks himself a judge.

I do allow that this case, and others of like nature, require more evidence to give them credit than ordinary cases do. You may therefore require more evidence in these, than in other cases; but it is absurd to say, that such cases admit no evidence, when the things in question are manifestly objects of sense.

I allow further, that the Gentleman has rightly stated the difficulty upon the foot of common prejudice; and that it arises from hence, that such cases appear to be contrary to the course of nature. But I desire to consider what this course of nature is. Every man, from the lowest countryman to the highest philosopher frames to himself from his experience and observation, a notion of a course of nature; and is ready to say of everything reported to him that contradicts his experience, that it is contrary to nature. But will the Gentleman say, that everything is impossible or even improbable, that contradicts the notion which men frame to themselves of the course of nature? I think he will not say it. And if he will, he must say that water can never freeze; for it is absolutely inconsistent with the notion which men have of the course of nature, who live in the warm climates. And hence it appears, that when men talk of the course of nature, they really talk of their own prejudices and imaginations; and that sense and reason are not so much concerned in the case as the Gentleman imagines. For I ask, Is it from the evidence of sense, or the evidence of reason that people of warm climates think it contrary to nature, that water should grow solid, and become ice? As for sense, they see indeed that water with them is always liquid; but none of their senses tell them that it can never grow solid. As for reason, it can never so inform them; for right reason can never contradict the truth of things. Our senses then inform us rightly what the usual course of things is; but when we conclude that things cannot be otherwise, we outrun the information of our senses, and the conclusion stands upon prejudice, and not upon reason. And yet such conclusions form what is generally called the course of nature. And when men upon proper evidence and informations admit things contrary to this presupposed course of nature, they do not, as the Gentleman expresses it, quit their own sense and reason; but, in truth, they quit their own mistakes and prejudices.

In the case before us, the case of the resurrection, the great difficulty arises from the like prejudice. We all know by experience that all men die, and rise no more; therefore we conclude, that for a dead man to rise to life again, is contrary to the course of nature. And certainly it is contrary to the uniform and settled course of things. But if we argue from hence that it is contrary and repugnant to the real laws of nature and absolutely impossible on that account, we argue without any foundation to support us either from our senses or our reason. We cannot learn from our eyes, or feeling, or any other sense, that it is impossible for a dead body to live again; if we learn it at all, it must be from our reason; and yet what one maxim of reason is contradicted by the supposition of a resurrection? For my own part; when I consider how I live; that all animal motions necessary to my life are independent of my will; that my heart beats without my consent and without my direction; that digestion and nutrition are performed by methods to which I am not conscious; that my blood moves in a perpetual round, which is contrary to all known laws of motion: I cannot but think, that the preservation of my life, in every moment of it, is as great an act of power, as is necessary to raise a dead man to life. And whoever so far reflects upon his own being as to acknowledge that he owes it to a superior power, must needs think, that the same power which gave life to senseless matter at first, and set all the springs and movements a-going at the beginning, can restore life to dead body. For surely it is not a greater thing to give life to a body once dead, than to a body that never was alive.

In the next place must be considered the difficulties which the gentleman has laid before you, with regard to the nature of Christ's body after the resurrection. He has produced some passages which which, he thinks, imply, that the body was not a real natural body, but a mere phantom, or apparition: and thence concludes, that there being no real object of sense, there can be no evidence in the case.

Presumptions are of no weight against positive evidence; and every account of the resurrection assures us, that the body of Christ was seen, felt, and handled by many persons; who were called upon by Christ so to do, that they might be assured that he had flesh and bones, and was not a mere spectre, as they, in their first surprize, imagined him to be. It is impossible that they who give this account, should mean, by anything they report, to imply that he had no real body; it is certain, then, that when the Gentleman makes use of what they say to this purpose, he uses their sayings contrary to their meaning: for it is not pretended that they say, that Christ had not a real human body after the resurrection; nor is it pretended they had any such thought, except only upon the first surprize of seeing him, and before they had examined him with their eyes and hands. But something they have said, which the Gentleman, according to his notions of philosophy, thinks, implies that the body was not real. To clear this point, therefore, I must lay before you the passages referred to, and consider how justly the Gentleman reasons from them.

The first passage relates to Mary Magdalene, who, the first time she saw Christ, was going to embrace his feet, as the custom of the country was: Christ says to her, [John 20:17] Touch me not, for I am not yet ascended to my Father; but go to my brethren and tell them, etc. Hence the gentleman concludes, that Christ's body was not such an one as would bear the touch. But how does he infer this? Is it from these words Touch me not? It cannot be: for thousands say it every day, without giving the least suspicion, that their bodies are not capable of being touched. The conclusion then must be built on those other words, For I have not yet ascended to my Father. but what have these words to do with the reality of his body? It might be real or not real, for anything that is here said. There is a difficulty in these words, and it may be hard to give the true sense of them; but there is no difficulty in seeing that they have no relation to the nature of Christ's body; for of his body nothing is said. The natural sense of the place as I collect, by comparing this passage with Matthew 28:9 is this. Mary Magdalene, upon seeing Jesus, fell at his feet, and laid hold of them and held them as if she meant never to let them go: Christ said to her, "Touch me not, or hang not about me now; you will have other opportunities of seeing me for I go not yet to my Father: lose no time then but go quickly with my message to my brethren." I am not concerned to support this particular interpretation of the passage; it is sufficient to my purpose, to show that the words cannot possibly relate to the nature of Christ's body one way or other.

The next passage relates to Christ's joining two of his disciples upon the road and conversing with them without being known by them: it grew dark, they pressed him to stay with them that night; he went in with them, broke bread, blessed it, and gave it them, and then they knew him; and immediately he disappeared.

The circumstance of disappearing, shall be considered under the next head, with other objections of the like kind. At present I shall only examine the other parts of this story, and inquire whether they afford any ground to conclude that the body of Christ was not a real one. Had this piece of history been related of any other person I think such suspicion could have risen. For what is there unnatural or uncommon in this account? Two men meet an acquaintance whom they thought dead: They converse with him for some time, without suspecting who he was; the very persuasion they were under that he was dead, contributed greatly to their not knowing him; besides, he appeared in a habit and form different from what he used when he conversed with them; appeared to them on a journey and walked with them side by side;

in which situation no one of the company has a full view of another: afterwards, when they were at supper together, and lights brought in, they plainly discerned who he was. Upon this occasion, the Gentleman asks what sort of witnesses these are? eye-witnesses? No; before supper they were eye-witnesses, says the Gentleman, that the person whom they saw was not Christ: and then he demands a reason for our rejecting the evidence of their sense when they did not know Christ, and insisting on it when they did.

It is no uncommon thing for men to catch themselves and others by such notable acute questions, and to be led by the sprightliness of their imagination out of the road of truth and common sense. I beg leave to tell the Gentleman a short story, and then to ask him his own question. A certain Gentleman who had been some years abroad happened in his return to England through Paris to meet his own sister there. She was not expecting to see him there, nor he to see her, they conversed together with other company, at a publick house, for great part of a day, without knowing each other. At last the Lady began to shew great signs of disorder; her color came and went, and the eyes of the company were drawn toward her; and then she cried out, Oh my brother! and was hardly held from fainting. Suppose now this Lady were to depose upon oath in a court of justice that she saw her brother at Paris; I would ask the Gentleman, Whether he would object to the evidence, and say, that she was as good an eye-witness that her brother was not there, as that he was; and demand of the court, why they rejected the evidence of her senses when she did not know her brother, and were ready to believe it when she did. When the question is answered in this case, I desire only to have the benefit of it in the case now before you. But if you shall be of opinion, that there was some extraordinary power used on this occasion, and incline to think that the expression, their eyes were holden, imports as much; then the case will fall under the next article. In which

We are to consider Christ's vanishing out of sight; his coming in and going out when the doors were shut; and such like passages; which, as they fall under one consideration, so I shall speak to them together.

But it is necessary first to see what the Apostles affirm distinctly in their accounts of these facts; for I think more has been said for them, than ever they said, or intended to say for themselves. In one place [Luke 24:31] it is said, he vanished out of their sight. Which translation is corrected in the margin of our Bibles thus: He ceased to be seen of them. And the original imports no more. It is said in another place, that the disciples being together, and the doors shut, Jesus came and stood in the midst of them. How he came, is not said; much less is it said that he came through the door, or the keyhole; and for anything that is said to the contrary, he might come in at the door, though the disciples saw not the door open, nor him, till he was in the midst of them. But the Gentleman thinks these passages prove that the disciples saw no real body, but an apparition. I am afraid that the Gentleman, after all his contempt of apparitions, and the superstition on which they are founded, has fallen into the snare himself, and is arguing upon no better principles than the common notions which the vulgar have of apparitions. Why else does he imagine these passages to be inconsistent with the reality of Christ's body? Is there no way for a real body to disappear? Try the experiment now; do but put out the candles, we shall all disappear. If a man falls asleep in the day-time, all things disappear to him; his senses are all locked up; and yet all things about him continue to be real, and his senses continue perfect. As shutting out all rays of light would make all things disappear; so intercepting the rays of light from any particular body, would make that disappear. Perhaps something like this was the case; or perhaps something else, which we know not. But, be the case what it will, the Gentleman's conclusion is founded on no principle of true philosophy: for it does not follow that a body is not real because I lose sight of it suddenly. I shall be told, perhaps, that this way of accounting for the passages is as wonderful, and as much out of the common course of things, as the other. Perhaps it is so; and what then? Surely the Gentleman does not expect, that, in order to prove the reality of the greatest miracle that ever was, I should shew that there was nothing miraculous in it, but that everything happened according to the ordinary course of things. My only concern is, to shew, that these passages do not infer, that the body of Christ after the resurrection was no real body. I wonder the Gentleman did not carry his argument a little further, and prove, that Christ, before his death, had no real body; for we read, that when the multitude would have thrown him down a precipice, he went through the midst of them unseen. Now, nothing happened after his resurrection more unaccountable than this that happened before it; and if the argument be good at all, it will be good to prove, that there never was such a man as Jesus in the world. Perhaps the gentleman may think that this is a little too much to prove: and if he does, I hope he will quit the argument in one case as well as in the other; for difference there is none.

Hitherto we have been called upon to prove the reality of Christ's body, and that it was the same after the resurrection that was before: but the next objection complains, that the body was too much the same with that which was buried; for the Gentleman thinks that it had the same mortal wounds open and uncured of which he died. His observation is grounded upon the words which Christ uses to Thomas: [John 20:27] Reach hither thy finger, and behold my hands; and reach hither thy hand and thrust it into my side. Is it here affirmed that Thomas did actually put his hand into his side, or so much as see his wounds fresh and bleeding? Nothing like it: but it is supposed from the words of Christ; for if he had no wounds, he would not have invited Thomas to probe them. Now, the meaning of Christ will best appear by an account of the occasion he had to use this speech. He had appeared to his disciples, in the absence of Thomas, and shewn them his hands and feet, which still had the marks of his crucifixion: the disciples report this to Thomas: he thought the thing impossible, and expressed his unbelief, as men are apt to do when they are positive, in a very extravagant manner: You talk, says he, of the prints of the nails in his hands and feet; for my part, says he, I'll never believe this thing, except I shall see in his hands the print of the nails, and put my finger into the print of the nails, and thrust my hand into his side. Now, in the first place, here is nothing said of open wounds; Thomas talks only of putting his finger into the print, that is, the scar of the nails, and thrusting his hand into his side. And, in common speech, to thrust an hand into any one's side does not signify to thrust it through the side into the bowels. Upon this interpretation of the words, which is a plain and natural one, the Gentleman's objection is quite gone. But suppose Thomas to mean what the Gentleman means; in that case the words of Christ are manifestly a severe reproach to him for his infidelity: Here, says Christ, are my hands and my side; take the satisfaction you require; thrust your fingers into my hands, your hand into my side; repeating to him his own words, and calling him to his own conditions; which, to a man beginning to see his extravagance, is of all rebukes the severest. Such forms of speech are used on many occasions, and are never understood to import that the thing proposed is proper, or always practicable. When the Grecian women reproached their sons with cowardice, and called to them as they were flying from the enemy, to come and hide themselves, like children as they were, in their mothers' wombs; he would be ridiculous who had asked the question, Whether the women really thought they could take their sons into their wombs again?

I have now gone through the objections which were necessarily to be removed before I could state the evidence in this case. I am sensible I have taken up too much of your time; but I have this to say in my excuse, That objections built on popular notions and prejudices, are easily conveyed to the mind in few words; and so conveyed, make strong impressions: but whoever answers the objections, must encounter all the notions to which they are allied, and to which they owe their strength; and it is well if with many words he can find admittance.

I come now to consider the evidence on which our belief of the resurrection stands. And here I am stopped again. A general exception is taken to the evidence, that it is imperfect, unfair; and a question is asked, Why did not Christ appear publickly to all the people, especially to the magistrates? Why were some witnesses culled and chosen out, and others excluded ? It may be sufficient perhaps to say, that where there are witnesses enow, no judge, no jury complains for want of more; and therefore, if the witnesses we have are sufficient, it is no objection that we have not others, and more. If three credible man attest a will, which are as many as the law requires, would any body ask, why all the town were not called to set their hands? But why were these witnesses culled and chosen out? Why? For this reason, that they might be good ones. Does not every wise men chuse proper witnesses to his deed and to his will? and does not a good choice of witnesses give strength to every deed? How comes it to pass, then, that the very thing which shuts out all suspicion in other cases should in this case only be of all others the most suspicious thing itself?

What reason there is to make any complaints on the behalf of the Jews, may be judged, in part, from what has already appeared. Christ suffered openly in their sight; and they were so well apprised of his prediction, that he should rise again, that they set a guard on his sepulchre; and from their guards they learned the truth. Every soldier was to them a witness of the resurrection of their own chusing. After this they had not one apostle,(which the Gentleman observes was the case of other people), but all the apostles, and many other witnesses with them, and in their power. The apostles testified the resurrection to them; not only to the people, but to the elders of Israel assembled in Senate: to support their evidence they were enabled to work, and did work miracles openly in the name of Christ. These people therefore have the least reason to complain; and had of all others the fullest evidence; and in some respects such as none but themselves could have, for they only were keepers of the sepulchre.I believe, if the gentleman was to chuse an evidence to his own satisfaction in a like case, he would desire no more, than to keep the sepulchre, with a sufficient number of guards.

But the argument goes further. It is said, that Jesus was sent with a special commission to the Jews; that he was their Messias; and as his resurrection was his main credential, he ought to have appeared publickly to the rulers of the Jews after his resurrection: that in doing otherwise, he acted like an ambassador pretending authority from his prince, but refusing to show his letters of credence.

I was afraid, when I suffered myself to be drawn into this argument, that I should be led into matters fitter to be decided by men of another profession, than by lawyers. But since there is no help now, I will lay before you what appears to me to be the natural and plain account of this matter; leaving it to others, who are better qualified, to give a fuller answer to the objection.

It appears to me, by the accounts we have of Jesus, that he had two distinct offices: one, as the Messias particularly promised to the Jews; another, as he was to be the great high priest of the world. With respect to the first office, he is called [Heb. 3:1] the apostle of the Hebrews; the [Rom. 15:8] minister of the circumcision; and says himself, [Matt 15:24] I am not sent, but unto the lost sheep of the house of Isreal. Accordingly, when he sent out his Apostles in his lifetime to preach, he expressly forbids them to go to the

Gentiles or Samaritans; but go, [Matt. 10:6] says he, to the lost sheep of the House of Israel. Christ continued in the discharge of this office during the time of his natural life, till he was finally rejected by the Jews. And it is observable, that the last time he spoke to the people according to St. Matthew's account, he solemnly took leave of them, and closed his commission. He had been long among them publishing glad tidings; but when all his preaching, all his miracles, had proved to be in vain, the last thing he did was, to denounce the woes they had brought on themselves. The 23d chapter of St. Matthew recites these woes; and at the end of them Christ takes this passionate leave of Jerusalem: "Oh, Jerusalem, Jerusalem, thou that killest the prophets and stonest them which are sent unto thee, how often would I have gathered thy children together, even as a hen gathereth her chickens under her wings, and ye would not! Behold, your house is left unto you desolate. For I say unto you, Ye shall not see me henceforth, till ye shall say, Blessed is he that cometh in the name of the Lord." It is remarkable, that this passage, as recorded by St. Matthew and St. Luke, twice over, is determined, by the circumstances, to refer to the near approach of his own death, and the extreme hatred of the Jews to him: and therefore those words, Ye shall not see me henceforth, are to be dated from the time of his death, and manifestly point out the end of his particular mission to them. From the making this declaration, as it stands in St. Matthew, his discourses are to his disciples, and they chiefly relate to the miserable and wretched condition of the Jews, which was now decreed, and soon to be accomplished. Let me now ask, Whether, in this state of things, any farther credentials of Christ's commission to the Jews could be demanded or expected? He was rejected, his commission was determined, and with it the fate of the nation was determined also: what use then of more credentials? As to appearing to them after his resurrection, he could not do it consistently with his own prediction, Ye shall see me no more, till ye shall say, Blessed is he that cometh in the name of the Lord. The Jews were not in this disposition after the resurrection, nor are they in it yet. The resurrection was the foundation of Christ's new commission, which extended to all the world. Then it was he declared, that all power was given unto him in heaven and in earth. Then he gave a new commission to his disciples, not restrained to the house of Israel, but to go and teach all nations. This prerogative the Jews had under this commission, that the gospel was every-where first offered to them; but in no other terms than it was offered to the rest of the world. Since then this commission, of which the resurrection was the foundation, extended to all the world alike; what ground is there to demand special and particular evidence to the Jews? The Emperor and the Senate of Rome were a much more considerable part of the world, than the chief priests and the synagogue; why does not the Gentleman object then, that Christ did not shew himself to Tiberius and his senate? And since all men have an equal right in this case,

Why may not the same demand be made for every country; nay, for every age? And then the Gentleman may bring the question nearer home; and ask, Why Christ did not appear in England in King George's reign? There is, to my apprehension, nothing more unreasonable, than to neglect and despise plain and sufficient evidence before us, and to sit down to imagine what kind of evidence would have pleased us; and then to make the want of such evidence an objection to the truth; which yet, if well considered, would be found to be well established.

The observation I have made upon the resurrection of Christ, naturally leads to another; which will help to account for the nature of the evidence we have in this great point. As the resurrection was the opening a new commission, in which all the world had an interest; so the concern naturally was, to have a proper evidence to establish this truth, and which should be of equal weight to all. This did not depend upon the satisfaction given to private persons, whether they were magistrates or not magistrates; but upon the conviction of those, whose office it was to be, to bear testimony to this truth in the world. In this sense the Apostles were chosen to be witnesses of the resurrection, because they were chosen to bear testimony to it in the world; and not because they only were admitted to see Christ after his resurrection: for the fact is otherwise. The gospel indeed, concerned to shew the evidence on which the faith of the world was to rest, is very particular in setting forth the ocular demonstration which the apostles had of the resurrection; and mentions others, who saw Christ after his resurrection, only accidentally, and as the thread of the history led to it. But yet it is certain, there were many others, who had this satisfaction, as well as the apostles. St. Luke tells us, that when Christ appeared to the eleven apostles, there were others with them [Luke 24:33]; who they were, or how many there were, he says not. But it appears in the Acts, when an apostle was to be chosen in the room of Judas; and the chief qualification required was, that he should be one capable of being a witness of the resurrection; that there were present an hundred and twenty so qualified [Acts 1. Compare vv. 15,21,22 together]. And Saint Paul says, that Christ after his rising was seen by 500 at once, many of whom were living when he appealed to their evidence. So that the Gentleman is mistaken, when he imagines that a few only were chosen to see Christ after he came from the grave. The truth of the case is, that, out of those who saw him, some were chosen to bear testimony to the world; and for that reason had the fullest demonstration of the truth, that they might be the better able to give satisfaction to others. And what was there in this conduct to complain of? what to raise any jealousy or suspicion?

As to the witnesses themselves, the first the Gentleman takes notice of, are the angels and the women. The mention of angels led naturally to apparitions: and the women were called poor silly women; and there is an end to their evidence. But to speak seriously: will the Gentleman pretend to prove, that there are no intelligent beings between God and man; or that they are not ministers of God; or that they were improperly employed in this great and wonderful work, the resurrection of Christ? Till some of these points are disproved we may be at rest; for the angels were ministers, and not witnesses of the resurrection. And it is not upon the credit of the poor silly women that we believe angels were concerned, but upon the report of those who wrote the gospels, who deliver it as a truth known to themselves, and not merely as a report taken from the women.

But for the women what shall I say? Silly as they were, I hope at least they had eyes and ears, and could tell what they heard and saw. In this case they tell no more. They report that the body was not in the sepulchre; but so far from reporting the resurrection; that they did not believe it, and were very anxious to find to what place the body was removed. Further they were not employed. For, I think, the Gentleman in another part observes rightly, that they were not sent to bear testimony to any people. But suppose them to be witnesses; suppose them to be improper ones; yet the evidence of the men surely is not the worse, because some wonen happened to see the same thing which they saw. And if men only must be admitted, of them we have enow to establish this truth.

I will not spend your time in enumerating these witnesses, or in setting forth the demonstration they had of the truth which they report. These things are well known. If you question their sincerity, they lived miserably, and died miserably, for the sake of this truth. And what greater evidence of sincerity can man give or require? And what is still more, they were not deceived in their expectation of being ill treated; for he who employed them, told them beforehand that the world would hate them, and treat them with contempt and cruelty.

But, leaving these weighty and well known circumstances to your own reflexion, I beg leave to lay before you another evidence, passed over in silence by the Gentleman on the other side. He took notice, that a resurrection was so extraordinary a thing, that no human evidence could support it. I am not sure that he is not in the right. If twenty men were to come into England with such a report from a distant country, perhaps they might not find twenty more here to believe their story. And I rather think the Gentleman may be in the right, because in the present case I see clearly, that the credit of the resurrection of Christ was not trusted to mere human evidence. To what evidence it was trusted, we find by his own declaration: The Spirit of truth, which proceedeth from the Father, he shall testify of me. And ye also (speaking to his apostles) shall bear witness, because ye have been with me from the beginning [John 15:26,27]. And therefore, though the apostles had conversed with him forty days after his resurrection, and had received his commission to go teach all nations; yet he expressly forbids them entering upon the work, till they should receive powers from above [Acts 1:14] And St. Peter explains the evidence of the resurrection in this manner: We (the apostles) are his witnesses of these things; and so is also the Holy Ghost, whom God hath given to them who obey him [Acts 5:32].

Now, what were the powers received by the apostles? Where they not the powers of wisdom and courage, by which they were enabled to appear before rulers and princes in the name of Christ; the power of miracles, even of raising the dead to life; by which they convinced the world, that God was with them in what they said and did? With respect to this evidence, St. John says, If we receive the witness of men, the witness of God is greater. [I John 5:9] Add to this, that the apostles had a power to communicate these gifts to believers. Can you wonder that men believed the reality of those powers of which they were partakers, and became conscious to themselves? With respect to these communicated powers, I suppose, St. John speaks, when he says, He that believeth on the Son of God hath the witness in himself: [I John 5:10] appealing, not to an inward testimony of the Spirit, in the sense of some modern enthusiasts; but to the powers of the Spirit, which believers received, and which were seen in the effects that followed.

It was objected, That the apostles separated themselves to the work of the ministry, and one went into one country, another to another; and, consequently, that the belief of the resurrection was originally received every where upon the testimony of one witness. I will not examine this fact. Suppose it to be so. But did this one witness go alone, when he was attended with the powers of heaven? Was not every blind man restored to sight, and every lame man to his feet, a new witness to the truth reported by the first? Besides, when the people of different countries came to compare notes, and found that they had all received the same account of Christ and of his doctrine; then surely the evidence of these distant witnesses thus united, became stronger than if they had told their story together: for twelve men separately examined form a much stronger proof for the truth of any fact, than twelve men agreeing together in one story.

If the same thing were to happen in our own time: if one or two were to come into England, and report that a man was raised from the dead; and, in consequence of it, teach nothing but that we ought to love God and our neighbors: if, to confirm their report, they should, before our eyes, cure the blind, the deaf, the lame, and even raise the dead to life: if, endued with all these powers, they should live in poverty and distress, and patiently submit to all that scorn, contempt, and malice could contrive to distress them; and at last sacrifice even their lives in justification of the truth of their report: if upon inquiry we should find, that all the countries in Europe had received the same account, supported by the same miraculous powers, attested in like manner by the sufferings, and confirmed by the blood of the witnesses: I would fain know what any reasonable man would do in this case? Would he despise such evidence? I think he would not. And whoever thinks otherwise, must say, that a resurrection, though in its own nature possible, is yet such a thing, in which we ought not to believe either God or man.

Judge. Have you done, Sir?

Mr. B. Yes, my Lord.

Judge. Go on, Mr. A., if you have anything to say in reply.

Mr. A. My Lord, I shall trouble you with very little. The objections and answers under this head, I shall leave to the judgment of the court; and beg leave only to make an observation or two upon the last part of the Gentleman's argument.

And first, with respect to the sufferings of the apostles and disciples of Jesus, and the argument drawn from thence for the truth of their doctrines and assertions, I beg leave to observe to you, that there is not a false religion or pretence in the world, but can produce the same authority, and show many instances of men who have suffered even to death for the truth of their several professions. If we consult only modern story we shall find Papists suffering for Popery, Protestants for their religion. And among Protestants every sect has had its martyrs; Puritans, Quakers, Fifth-monarchy men. In Henry VIII's time England saw both Popish and Protestant martyrs; in Queen Mary's reign the rage fell upon Protestants; in Queen Elizabeth's Papists and Puritans were called sometimes, though rarely, to this trial. In later times, sometimes churchmen, sometimes dissenters were persecuted. What must we say, then? All these sufferers had not truth with them; and yet, if there be any weight in this argument from suffering they have all the right to plead it.

But I may be told, perhaps, that men by their sufferings, though they do not prove their doctrines to be true, yet prove at least their own sincerity: as if it were a thing impossible for men to dissemble at the point of death. Alas! how many instances are there of men's denying facts plainly proved, asserting facts plainly disproved, even with the rope around their necks? Must all such pass for innocent sufferers, sincere men? If not, it must be allowed, that a man's word at the point of death is not always to be relied on.

Another observation I would make, is with respect to the evidence of the Spirit, on which so much stress is laid. It has been hitherto insisted on, that the resurrection was a matter of fact, and such a fact as was capable and proper to be supported by the evidence of sense. How comes it about, that this evidence, this which is the proper evidence, is given up as insufficient, and a new improper evidence introduced? Is it not surprising, that one great miracle should want an hundred more to prove it? Every miracle is itself an appeal to sense, and therefore admits no evidence but that of sense. And there is no connexion between a miracle done this year and last year. It does not follow, therefore, because Peter cured a lame man, (allowing the fact), that therefore Christ rose from the dead.

But allowing the Gentleman all he demands, what is to us? They who had the witness within them, did perhaps very well to consult, and to take his word; but how am I, or others, who have not this witness is us, the better for it? If the first ages of the church saw all the wonders related by the Gentleman, and believed, it shews at least, in his opinion, that this strong evidence was necessary to create the belief he requires; why then does he require this belief of us, who have not this strong evidence?

Judge. Very well. Gentlemen of the jury, You have heard the proofs and arguments on both sides, and it is now your part to give a verdict.

Here the Gentlemen whispered together, and the Foreman stood up.

Foreman. My Lord, The case has been long, and consists of several articles; therefore the jury hope you will give them your directions.

Judge. No, no; you are very able to judge without my help.

Mr. A. My Lord, Pray consider, you appointed this meeting and chose your office. Mr. B. and I have gone through our parts, and have some right on your doing your part.

Mr. B. I must join, Sir, in that request.

Judge. I have often heard, that all honour has a burden attending it; but I did not suspect it in this office, which I conferred upon myself. But, since it must be so, I will recollect, and lay before you, as well as I can, the substance of the debate.

Gentlemen of the jury, The question before you, is Whether the witnesses of the resurrection of Christ are guilty of giving false evidence, or no?

Two sorts of objections, or accusations, are brought against them. One charges fraud and deceit on the transaction itself; the other charges the evidence as forged, and insufficient to support the credit of so extraordinary an event.

There are also three periods of time to be considered.

The first takes in the ministry of Christ, and ends at his death. During this period the fraud is supposed to be contrived.

The second reaches from his death to his resurrection. During this period the fraud is supposed to be executed.

The third begins from the resurrection, and takes in the whole ministry of the apostles. And here the evidence they gave the world for this fact is the main consideration.

As to the first period of time, and the fraud charged upon Jesus, I must observe to you, that this charge had no evidence to support it; all the facts reported of Jesus stand in full contradiction to it. To suppose, as the council did, that this fraud might possibly appear, if we had any Jewish books written at the time, is not to bring proof, but to wish for proof: for, as it was rightly observed on the other side, how does Mr. A. know there were any such books? And since they are lost, how does he know what was in them? Were such books extant, they might probably prove beyond dispute the facts recorded in the gospels.

You were told, that the Jews were a very superstitious people, much addicted to prophecy; and particularly, that they had a strong expectation about the time that Christ appeared, to have a victorious prince rise among them. This is laid as the ground of suspicion; and, in fact, many imposters, you are told, set up upon these notions of the people; and thence it is inferred, that Christ built his scheme upon the strength of these popular prejudices. But when this fact came to be examined on the other side, it appeared, that Christ was so far from falling in with these notions, and abusing the credulity of the people, that it was his main point, to correct these prejudices, to oppose these superstitions; and by these very means he fell into disgrace with his countrymen, and suffered as one who, in their opinion, destroyed the Law and the Prophets. With respect to temporal power, so far was he from aiming at it, that he refused it when offered: so far from giving any hopes of it to his disciples, that he invited men upon quite different terms: To take up the cross, and follow him. And it is observable, that, after he had foretold his death and resurrection, he continued to admonish his disciples of the evils they were to suffer; to tell them, that the world would hate them, and abuse them; which surely to common sense has no appearance that he was then contriving a cheat, or encouraging his disciples to execute it.

But as ill supported as this charge is, there was no avoiding it; it was necessity and not choice, which drove the Gentleman to it: for since Christ had foretold his resurrection, if the whole was a cheat, he certainly was conscious to it, and consequently the plot was laid in his own time. And yet the supposing Christ conscious to such a fraud in these circumstance, is contrary to all probability. It is very improbable, that he, or any man, should, without any temptation, contrive a cheat to take place after his death. And if this could be supposed, it is highly improbable that he should give publick notice of it, and thereby put all men on their guard; especially considering there were only a few women, and twelve men, of low fortunes, and mean education, to conduct the plot, and the whole power of the Jews and Romans to oppose it.

Mr. A. seemed sensible of these difficulties, and therefore would have varied the charge, and have made Christ an enthusiast, and his disciples only cheats. This was not properly moved, and therefore not debated; for which reason I shall pass it over with this short observation; that enthusiasm is as contrary to the whole character and conduct of Christ, as even fraud is. Besides, this imagination, if allowed, goes only to Christ's own part; and leaves the charge of fraud, in its full extent, upon the management from the time of his death; and therefore is of no use, unless the fraud afterwards be apparent. For if there really was a resurrection, it will sufficiently answer the charge of enthusiasm.

I pass on to the second period, to consider what happened between the death and resurrection of Christ. And here it agreed that Christ died, and was buried. So far then there was no fraud.

For the better understanding the charge here, we must recollect a material circumstance reported by one of the evangelists; which is this: After Christ was buried, the chief priests and Pharisees came to Pilate, the Roman governor, and informed him, that this deceiver (meaning Jesus) had in his lifetime foretold, that he would rise again after three days; that they suspected his disciples would steal away the body, and pretend a resurrection; and then the last error would be worse than the first. They therefore desire a guard to watch the sepulchre, to prevent all fraud. They had one granted; accordingly they placed a watch on the sepulchre, and sealed up the stone at the mouth of it.

What the event of this case was, the same writer tells us. The guards saw the stone removed by angels, and for fear they became as dead men: when they came to the city, they reported to the chief priests what had happened: a council is called, and a resolution taken to bribe the soldiers to say, that the body was stolen while they were asleep; and the council undertook to excuse the soldiers to Pilate, for their negligence in falling asleep when they were on duty.

Thus the fact stands in the original record. Now, the council for Woolston maintains, that the story reported by the soldiers, after they had been bribed by the chief priests, contains the true account of this pretended resurrection.

The Gentleman was sensible of a difficulty in his way, to account for the credit which the Jews gave to the prediction of Christ; for if, as he pretends, they knew him to be an impostor, what reason had they to take any notion of his prediction? And therefore, that very caution in this case betrayed their concern, and shewed, that they were not satisfied that his pretensions were groundless. To obviate this, he says, That they had discovered before, one great cheat in the case of Lazarus, and therefore were suspicious of another in this case. He was answered, That the discovery of a cheat in the case before mentioned, ought rather to have set them at ease, and made them quite secure as to the event of the prediction. In reply he says, That the chief priests, however satisfied of the cheat themselves, had found that it prevailed among the people; and, to secure the people from being further imposed on, they used the caution they did.

This is the substance of the argument on both sides.

I must observe to you, that this reasoning from the case of Lazarus has no foundation in history. There is no pretence for saying, that the Jews in this whole affair had any particular regard to the raising of Lazarus. And if they had any such just suspicion, why was it not mentioned at the trial of Christ? There was then an opportunity of opening the whole fraud, and undeceiving the people. The Jews had a plain law for punishing a false prophet; and what could be a stronger conviction, than such a cheat made manifest? Why then was this advantage lost?

The Gentleman builds this observation on these words, So the last error shall be worse than the first. But is there here anything said about Lazarus? No. The words are a proverbial form of speech, and probably were used without relation to any particular case. But if a particular meaning must be assigned, it is more probable, that the words being used to Pilate, contained a reason applicable to him. Now, Pilate had been drawn in to consent to the crucifixion, for fear the Jews should set up Jesus to be their King in opposition to Caesar; therefore say the chief priests to him, If once the people believe him to be risen from the dead, the last error will be worse than the first; i.e. they will be more inclined and encouraged to rebel against the Romans than ever. This is a natural sense of the words, as they are used to move the Roman governor to allow them a guard. Whether Lazarus were dead or alive; whether Christ came to destroy the Law and the Prophets, or to establish or confirm them, was of little moment to Pilate. It is plain, he was touched by none of these considerations; and refused to be concerned in the affair of Christ, till he was alarmed with the suggestions of danger to the Roman state. This was the first fear that moved him; must not therefore the second now suggested to him be of the same kind?

The next circumstance to be considered, is that of the seal upon the stone of the sepulchre. The council for Woolston supposes an agreement between the Jews and disciples about setting this seal. But for this agreement there is no evidence; nay, to suppose it, contradicts the whole series of the history, as the Gentleman on the other side observed. I will not enter into the particulars of this debate; for it is needless. The plain natural account given of this matter, shuts out all other suppositions. Mr. B. observed to you, that the Jews having a guard, set the seal to prevent any combination among the guards to deceive them: which seems a plain and satisfactory account. The council for W. replies, Let the use of the seals be what they will, it is plain they were broken; and if they were used as a check upon the Roman soldiers, then probably they consented to the fraud: and then it is easily understood how the body was removed.

I must observe to you here, that this suspicion agrees neither with the account given by the evangelist, nor with the story set about by the Jews; so that it is utterly unsupported by any evidence.

Nor has it any probability in it. For what could move Pilate, and the Roman soldiers, to propagate such a cheat? He had crucified Christ, for no other reason, but for fear the people would revolt from the Romans; perhaps too he consented to place a guard upon the sepulchre, to put an end to the people's hope in Jesus: and is it likely at last that he was consenting to a cheat, to make the people believe him risen from the dead; the thing, of all others, which he was obliged, as his apprehensions were, to prevent?

The next circumstance insisted on as a proof of the fraud, is, that Jesus rose from the dead before the time he had appointed. Mr. A. supposes that the disciples hastened the plot, for fear of falling in with multitudes, who waited only for the appointed time to be at the sepulchre, and to see with their own eyes. He was answered, That the disciples were not, could not be concerned, or be present at moving the body; that they were dispersed, and lay concealed for fear of the Jews: that hastening the plot, was of no use; for the resurrection happened whilst the guards were at the sepulchre; who were probably enow to prevent violence; certainly enow to discover it, if any were used.

This difficulty then rests merely upon the reckoning of the time. Christ died on Friday, rose early on Sunday. The question is, Whether this was rising the third day, according to the prediction? I will refer the authorities made use of in this case to your memory, and add only one observation, to shew that it was indeed the third day, according as the people of the country reckoned. When Christ talked with the two disciples who knew him not, they gave him an account of his own crucifixion, and their disappointment; and tell him, Today is the third day since these things were done [Luke24:21]. Now, this conversation was on the very day of the resurrection. And the disciples thought of nothing less than answering an objection against the resurrection, which as yet they did not believe. They recount only a matter of fact, and reckon the time according to the usage of their country, and call the day of the resurrection the third day from the crucifixion; which is a plain evidence, in what manner the Jews reckoned in this and like cases.

As the objections in this case are founded upon the story reported by the Jews, and the Roman soldiers, Mr. B. in his answer, endeavored to shew, from some historical passages, that the Jews themselves did not believe the story.

His first argument was, That the Jews never questioned the disciples for this cheat, and the share they had in it, when they had them in their power. And yet who sees not that it was very much in their purpose so to do? To this there is no reply.

The second argument was from the treatment St. Paul had from King Agrippa, and his saying to St. Paul, Almost thou persuadest me to be a Christian: A speech which he reckons could not be made by a prince, to one concerned in carrying out a known cheat. To this the Gentleman replies, That Agrippa never did become a Christian; and that no great stress is to be laid upon his compliance to his prisoner. But allowing that there was something of humanity and civility in the expression, yet such civility could hardly be paid to a known impostor. There is a propriety even in civility. A prince may be civil to a rebel; but he will hardly compliment him for his loyalty: he may be civil to a poor sectary; but if he knows him to be a cheat, he will scarcely compliment him with hopes that he will be of his party.

The third argument was from the advice given by Gamaliel to the council of the Jews, to let the apostles alone, for fear they themselves should be found to fight against God: A supposition which the Gentleman thinks absolutely inconsistent with his, or the council's being persuaded, that the apostles were guilty of any fraud in managing the resurrection of Christ.

The Gentleman replies, That Gamaliel's advice respected only the numbers of people deceived; and was a declaration of his opinion, that it was not prudent to come to extremities till the people were in a better temper. This deserves consideration.

First, I observe, that Gamaliel's words are express, Lest ye be found to fight against God; which reason respects God, and not the people. And the suppostion is, that the hand of God might possibly be in this work: A saying which could not have come from him, or have been received by the council, if they had believed the resurrection to have been a cheat.

Secondly, It is remarkable, that the miracles wrought by the apostles after the death of Christ, those especially which occasioned the calling of this council, had a much greater effect upon the Jews, than even the miracles of Christ himself. They held out against all the wonders of Christ, and were perpetually plotting his death, not doubting but that would put an end to all their trouble: but when, after his death, they saw the same powers continue with the apostles, they saw no end of the affair, but began to think in earnest there might be more in it than they were willing to believe. And, upon the report made to them of the apostle's works, they make serious reflexion, and doubted whereunto this would grow. And though in their anger and vexation of heart they thought of desperate remedies, and were for killing the apostles also; yet they hearkened willing to Gamaliel's advice; which at another time might have been dangerous to the adviser. So that it appears from the history, that the whole council had the same doubt that Gamaliel had, that possibly the hand of God might be in this thing. And could the Jews, if they had manifestly discovered the cheat of the resurrection a little time before, have entertained such a suspicion?

The last period commences at the resurrection, and takes in the evidence upon which the credit of this fact stands.

The council for Woolston, among other difficulties, started one, which, if well grounded, excludes all evidence out of this case. The resurrection being a thing out of the course of nature, he thinks the testimony of nature, held forth to us in her constant method of working, a stronger evidence against the possibility of a resurrection, than any human evidence can be for the reality of one.

In answer to this, it is said, on the other side,

First, That a resurrection is a thing to be judged of by mens senses; and this cannot be doubted. We all know when a man is dead; and should he come to life again, we might judge whether he was alive or no, by the very same means by which we judge those about us to be living men.

Secondly, That the notion of a resurrection, contradicts no one principle of right reason, interferes with no law of nature: and that whoever admits that God gave man life at first, cannot possibly doubt of his power to restore it when lost.

Thirdly, That appealing to the settled course of nature, is referring the matter in dispute, not to rules or maxims of reason and true philosophy, but to the prejudices and mistakes of men; which are various and infinite, and differ sometimes according to the climate men live in; because men form a notion of nature from what they see: and therefore in cold countries all men judge it to be according to the course of nature for water to freeze; in warm countries they judge it to be unnatural. Consequently, that it is not enough to prove anything to be contrary to the laws of nature, to say that it is usually, or constantly, to our observation, otherwise. And therefore, though men in the ordinary course die, and do not rise again, (which is certainly a prejudice against the belief of a resurrection); yet is it not an argument against the possibility of a resurrection?

Another objection was against the reality of the body of Christ after it came from the grave. These objections are founded upon such passages as report his appearing or disappearing to the eyes of his disciples at pleasure; his coming in among them when the doors were shut; his forbidding some to touch him, his inviting others to do it; his having the very wounds whereof he died, fresh and open in his body, and the like. Hence the council concluded, that it was no real body, which was sometimes visible, sometimes invisible; sometimes capable of being touched, sometimes incapable.

On the other side it was answered, That many of these objections are founded on a mistaken belief of the passages referred to; particularly of the passage in which Christ is thought to forbid Mary Magdalene to touch him; of another, in which he calls to Thomas to examine his wounds; and probably of a third, relating to Christ's conversation with his disciples on the road, without being known by them.

As to other passages which relate his appearing and disappearing, and coming in when the doors were shut, it is said, that no conclusion can be drawn from them against the reality of Christ's body: that these things might happen many ways, and yet the body be real; which is the only point to which the present objection extends: that there might be in this, and probably was, something miraculous; but nothing more wonderful than what happened on another occasion in his lifetime, where the Gentleman who makes the objection allows him to have had a real body.

I mention these things but briefly, just to bring the course of the argument to your remembrance.

The next objection is taken from hence, That Christ did not appear publickly to the people, and particularly to the chief priests and rulers of the Jews. It is said, that his commission related to them in an especial manner; and that it appears strange, that the main proof of his mission, the resurrection, should not be laid before them; but that witnesses should be picked and culled to see this mighty wonder. This is the force of the objection.

To which it is answered, First, That the particular commission to the Jews expired at the death of Christ; and therefore the Jews had, on this account, no claim for any particular evidence. And it is insisted, that Christ, before his death, declared, the Jews should not see him, till they were better disposed to receive him.

Secondly, That as the whole world had a concern in the resurrection of Christ, it was necessary to prepare a proper evidence for the whole world; which was not to be done by any particular satisfaction given to the people of the Jews, or their rulers.

Thirdly, That as to the chosen witnesses, it is a mistake to think that they were chosen as the only persons to see Christ after the resurrection; and that in truth many others did see him: but that the witnesses were chosen as proper persons to bear testimony to all people; an office to which many others who did see Christ, were not particularly commissioned. That making choice of proper and credible witnesses, was so far from being a ground of just suspicion, that it is in all cases the most proper way to exclude suspicion..

The next objection is pointed against the evidence of the angels, and the women. It is said, That history reports, that the women saw young men at the sepulchre; that they were advanced into angels, merely through the fear and superstition of the women: that, at the best, this is but a story of an apparition; a thing in times of ignorance much talked of, but in the days of knowledge never heard of.

In answer to this, it is said, That the angels are not properly reckoned among the witnesses of the resurrection; they were not in the number of the chosen witnesses, or sent to bear testimony in the world: that they were indeed ministers of God appointed to attend the resurrection: that God has such ministers, cannot be reasonably doubted; nor can it be objected, that they were improperly employed, or below their dignity, in attending on the resurrection of Christ: that we believe them to be angels, not on the report of the women, but upon the credit of the evangelist who affirms it: that what is said of apparitions on this occasion, may pass for wit and ridicule, but yields not reason or argument.

The objection to the women was, I think, only that they were women; which was strengthened by calling them silly women.

It was answered, That women have eyes and ears as well as men, and can tell what they see and hear. And it happened in this case, that the women were so far from being credulous, that they believed not the angels, and hardly believed their own report. However, that the women are none of the chosen witnesses; and if they were, the evidence of the men cannot be set aside, because women saw what they saw..

This is the substance of the objections and the answers.

The council for the apostles insisted further, That they gave the greatest assurance to the world that possibly could be given, of their sincere dealing, by suffering all kinds of hardship, and at last death itself, in confirmation of the truth of their evidence.

The council for Woolston, in reply to this, told you, That all religions, whether true or false, had had their martyrs; that no opinion, however absurd, can be named, but some have been content to die for it; and then concluded, that suffering is no evidence of the truth of the opinions for which men suffer.

To clear this matter to you, I must observe how this case stands. You have heard often, in the course of this argument, that the apostles were witnesses chosen to bear testimony to the resurrection; and, for that reason, had the fullest evidence themselves of the truth of it; not merely by seeing Christ once or twice after his death, but by frequent conversations with him for forty days together, before his ascension. That this was their proper business, appears plainly from history; where we find, that to ordain an apostle, was the same thing as ordaining one to be a witness of the resurrection.[Acts 1:22] If you look further, to the preaching of the apostles, you will find this was the great article insisted on [Acts 2:22, 3:15, 4:10, 5:30]. And St. Paul knew the weight of this article, and the necessity of teaching it, when he said, If Christ be not risen, our faith is vain. You see, then, that the thing which the apostles testified, and the thing for which they suffered, was the truth of the resurrection; which is a mere matter of fact.

Consider now how the objection stands. The council for Woolston tells you, that it is common for men to die for false opinions; and he tells you nothing but the truth. But even in those cases their suffering is an evidence of their sincerity; and it would be very hard to charge men who die for the doctrine they profess, with insincerity in the profession. Mistaken they may be; but every mistaken man is not a cheat. Now, if you will allow the suffering of the apostles to prove their sincerity, which you cannot well disallow; and consider that they died for the truth of a matter of fact which they had seen themselves, you will perceive how strong the evidence is in this case. In doctrines, and matters of opinion, men mistake perpetually; and it is no reason for me to take up with another man's opinion, because I am persuaded he is sincere in it. But when a man reports to me an uncommon fact, yet such an one as in its own nature is a plain object of sense; if I believe him not, it is not because I suspect his eyes, or his sense of feeling, but merely because I suspect his sincerity: for if I was to see the same thing myself, I should believe myself; and therefore my suspicion does not arise from the inability of human senses to judge in the case, but from a doubt of the sincerity of the reporter. In such cases, therefore, there wants nothing to be proved, but only the sincerity of the reporter: and since voluntary sufferings for the truth, is at least a proof of sincerity; the sufferings of the apostles for the truth of the resurrection, is a full and unexceptionable proof.

The council for Woolston was sensible of this difference; and therefore he added, that there are many instances of men's suffering and dying in an obstinate denial of the truth of facts plainly proved. This observation is also true. I remember a story of a man who endured with great constancy all the tortures of the rack, denying the fact with which he was charged. When he was asked afterwards, how he could hold out against all the tortures? He answered, I had painted a gallows upon the toe of my shoe, and when the rack stretched me, I looked on the gallows, and bore the pain, to save my life. This man denied a plain fact, under great torture; but you see a reason for it. In other cases, when criminals persist in denying their crimes, they often do it, and there is a reason to suspect they do it always, in hopes of a pardon or reprieve. But what are these instances to the present purpose? All these men suffer against their will, and for their crimes; and their obstinacy is built on the hope of escaping, by moving the compassion of the government. Can the Gentleman give any instances of persons who died willingly in attestation of a false fact? We have had in England some weak enough to die for the Pope's supremacy; but do you think a man could be found to die in proof of the Pope's being actually on the throne of England?

Now, the apostles died in asserting the truth of Christ's resurrection. It was always in their power to quit their evidence and save their lives. Even their bitterest enemies, the Jews, required no more of them than to be silent. [Acts 4:17, 5:28] Others have denied facts, or asserted facts, in hopes of saving their lives, when they were under sentence of death: but these men attested a fact at the expence of their lives, which they might have saved by denying the truth. So that between criminals dying, and denying plain facts, and the apostles dying for their testimony, there is this material difference: criminals deny the truth in hopes of saving their lives; the apostles willingly parted with their lives, rather than deny the truth.

We are come now to the last, and indeed the most weighty consideration.

The council for the apostles having in the course of the argument allowed, that more evidence is required to support the credit of the resurrection, it being a very extraordinary event, than is necessary in common cases, in the latter part of his defence sets forth the extraordinary evidence upon which this fact stands. That is, the evidence of the Spirit, the Spirit of wisdom and power, which was given to the apostles, to enable them to confirm their testimony by signs and wonders, and mighty works. This part of the argument was well argued by the Gentleman, and I need not repeat all he said.

The council for Woolston, in his reply, made two objections to this evidence.

The first was this: That the resurrection having all along been pleaded to be a matter of fact, and an object of sense, to recur to miracles for the proof of it, is to take it out of its proper evidence, the evidence of sense; and to rest it upon a proof which cannot be applied to it: for seeing one miracle, he says, is no evidence that another miracle was wrought before it; as healing a sick man, is no evidence that a dead man was raised to life.

To clear this difficulty, you must consider by what train of reasoning miracles come to be proofs in any case. A miracle of itself proves nothing, unless this only, that there is a cause equal to the producing the effect we see. Suppose you should see a man raise one from the dead, and he should go away and say nothing to you, you would not find that any fact, or any proposition, was proved or disproved by this miracle. But should he declare to you, in the name of him, by whose power the miracle was wrought, that image-worship was unlawful, you would then be possessed of a proof against image-worship. But how? Not because the miracle proves anything as to the point itself, but because the man's declaration is authorised by him who wrought the miracle in confirmation of his doctrine; and therefore miracles are directly a proof of the authority of persons, and not of the truth of things.

To apply this to the present case: If the apostles had wrought miracles, and said nothing of the resurrection, the miracles would have proved nothing about the resurrection one way or another. But when as eye-witnesses they attested the truth of the resurrection, and wrought miracles to confirm their authority; the miracles did not directly prove the resurrection; but they confirmed and established beyond all suspicion the proper evidence, the evidence of eye-witnesses. So that here is no change of the evidence from proper to improper; the fact still rests upon the evidence of sense, confirmed and strengthened by the authority of the Spirit. If a witness calls in his neighbors to attest his veracity, they prove nothing as to the fact in question, but only confirm the evidence of the witness. The case here is the same; though between the authorities brought in confirmation of the evidence, there is no comparison.

The second objection was, That this evidence, however good it may be in its kind, is yet nothing to us. It was well, the Gentleman says, for those who had it; but what is that to us, who have it not?

To adjust this difficulty, I must observe to you, that the evidence now under consideration, was not a private evidence of the Spirit, or any inward light, like to that which the Quakers in our time pretend to; but an evidence appearing in the manifest and visible works of the Spirit: and this evidence was capable of being transmitted, and actually has been transmitted to us upon unquestionable authority. And to allow the evidence to have been good in the first ages, and not in this, seems to be to be a contradiction to the rules of reasoning: for if we see enough to judge that the first ages had reason to believe, we must needs see at the same time, that it is reasonable for us also to believe. As the present question only relates to the nature of the evidence, it was not necessary to produce from history the instances to shew in how plentiful a manner this evidence was granted to the church. Whoever wants this satisfaction, may easily have it.

Gentlemen of the jury, I have laid before you the substance of what has been said on both sides. You are now to consider of it, and to give your verdict.

The jury consulted together, and the Foreman rose up.

Foreman. My Lord, We are ready to give our verdict.

Judge. Are you all agreed?

Jury. Yes.

Judge. Who shall speak for you?

Jury. Our Foreman.

Judge. What say you? Are the apostles guilty of giving false evidence in the case of the resurrection of Jesus, or not guilty?

Foreman. Not guilty.

Judge. Very well. And now, Gentlemen, I resign my commission and am your humble servant.

The company rose up, and were beginning to pay their compliments to the judge and the council; but were interrupted by a Gentleman, who went up to the judge, and offered him a fee. What's this? Says the judge. A fee, Sir, said the Gentleman. A fee to a judge is a bribe, said the judge. True, Sir, said the Gentleman; but you have resigned your commission, and will not be the first judge who has come from the bench without any diminution of honour. Now, Lazarus's case is to come on next, and this fee is to retain you on his side. There followed a confused noise of all speaking together, to persuade the judge to take the fee: but as the trial had lasted longer than I expected, and I had lapsed the time of an appointment for business, I was forced to slip away; and whether the judge was prevailed on to undertake the cause of Lazarus, or no, I cannot say.

FINIS

Milton Keynes UK
Ingram Content Group UK Ltd.
UKHW030743071024
449371UK00006B/596